Great Jobs

for

Political Science Majors

Mark Rowh

SERIES DEVELOPERS AND CONTRIBUTING AUTHORS
Stephen E. Lambert
Julie Ann DeGalan

VGM Career Horizons
NTC/Contemporary Publishing Group

Library of Congress Cataloging-in-Publication Data

Rowh, Mark.
    Great jobs for political science majors / Mark Rowh.
       p.   cm. — ("Great jobs")
    Includes index.
    ISBN 0-8442-4724-3
     1. Political science—Vocational guidance—United States.
  2. College graduates—Employment—United States.   3. Occupations—United States. I. Title. II. Series.
  JA88.U6R68   1998
  320′.023′73—dc21   98-7263
                                          CIP

Published by VGM Career Horizons
A division of NTC/Contemporary Publishing Group, Inc.
4255 West Touhy Avenue, Lincolnwood (Chicago), Illinois 60646-1975 U.S.A.
Copyright © 1999 by NTC/Contemporary Publishing Group, Inc.
Printed in the United States of America
International Standard Book Number: 0-8442-4724-3
98   99   00   01   02   03   LB   6   5   4   3   2

To David Rowh and all the young men and women who have
served their country through the AmeriCorps program

CONTENTS

Acknowledgments

The author offers grateful thanks to the following for their cooperation in providing information for this book:

Alzheimer's Association

American Political Science Association

Canadian Political Science Association

Case Western Reserve University

Midwest Political Science Association

Rose Miskowiec

National Association of Schools of Public Affairs and
   Administration

Northwestern University

The University of Calgary

The University of Minnesota

U.S. Department of Labor

Vanderbilt University

Virginia Department of Education

POLITICAL SCIENCE: PATHWAY TO SUCCESS

f you've studied political science, you've learned just how important government and political institutions are to modern life. Without government and the political processes that support it, our culture would dissolve into anarchy. Sure, government can be intrusive, inflexible, cumbersome, and expensive. But it also serves as the foundation for law, commerce, personal freedom, and other fundamental components of a civilized society.

Of course, as a political science major you already know about the importance of the political realm. But you may not realize that those who study political science enjoy a wide range of career options.

Perhaps you chose a major in political science because you hope to attend law school. That is a perfectly valid reason, and many students use an undergraduate degree with a major in political science as the first step toward attending law school and becoming attorneys.

On the other hand, maybe you haven't really considered the law school option. If that is the case, don't overlook this opportunity. Law school isn't for everyone, and neither is a legal career. But as a political science major, this is one direction you might want to examine.

Or let's go in another direction. Perhaps you have thought about going into politics. If so, what academic preparation could serve you better than political science? Maybe someday you'll be running for the state legislature, the U.S. Congress, the governorship of your state, or an even higher position. Who knows? Maybe a political science degree will help you win a ticket to Air Force One!

Then again, maybe you haven't considered a political career. Given your interest in government and the credentials a political science degree provides, such a path is something you might want to explore. Or you might want to think about a government service career, where you are employed by the federal government or a state or local government agency.

Or how about teaching? Or journalism? Or business? The truth is, a political science background can lead in many different directions.

A FIELD WITH FEW LIMITS

If you major in political science, does that make you a political scientist? Actually, completing a major in this field doesn't lead to just one end result. The range of jobs performed by political science majors is impressively diverse.

In its brochure "Political Science: An Ideal Liberal Arts Major," the American Political Science Association lists the following examples of actual positions held by political science graduates:

Administrative assistant in state sales tax bureau

Advisor to chairman of state Energy Commission

Assistant budget examiner

Assistant deputy secretary to governor

Associate research director, advertising firm

Attorney

Campaign finance analyst

Chief, county Bureau of Labor and Training

Chief of staff, committee, U.S. House of Representatives

Chief, state general government services office

CIA, advanced concepts staff, Office of Research and Development

City housing administrator

City housing manager

City office of planning and community development, staff assistant

City project coordinator

Commissioner, state Department of Human Services

Consultant

Corporate economist

Corporate international analyst

Corporate manager of environmental and regulatory affairs

Corporate public affairs officer

Corporate senior advisor for governmental relations

Corporate state legislative issues manager

County clerk

County council member

Credit research manager

Deputy manager, political risk insurance division

Deputy secretary for administration, state Department of Welfare

Deputy secretary to governor

Director, cost containment, insurance company

Director, division of policy studies

Director, political information products

Director, public affairs

Executive director, special interest association

FAA personnel officer

Federal commission senior policy analyst

Financial consultant

Foundation president

HUD, senior legislative specialist

Information manager, corporate planning department

International research specialist

Investigator, OPM

Investment officer

Labor relations specialist

Librarian

Library of Congress, specialist

Management analyst

Manager of political programs

Mayor's office, legislative coordinator

Member of state assembly

Minister for development

Plans and review officer, U.S. Information Agency

Principal secretary to prime minister

Private foundation program director

Program evaluator

Public affairs research analyst

Publisher

Research supervisor

Senior advisor, Department of Treasury

Senior criminologist

Senior editor

Senior employee relations analyst

State department, director, policy and coordination

State department officer

State personnel officer

State senator

Supervisor, state Department of Education

Survey analyst

Television network, director of surveys

Traffic courts coordinator

U.S. Army, strategic planning specialist

U.S. consulate, principal officer

U.S. Supreme Court, judicial fellow

University president

Veterans administration adjudication unit chief

Vice president, account executive

Vice president, account group head

Vice president, market research

These are just *some* of the jobs held by political science grads. In government, law, business, education, and the nonprofit sector, among other areas, those with political science backgrounds can flourish.

THE IDEAL POLITICAL SCIENCE GRADUATE

The ideal political science graduate might be a specialist. He or she might have concentrated in a specific field of study such as international relations, preparing to perform a narrow range of duties. Or, the ideal political science grad could be a generalist. This person might be prepared to take on almost any entry-level position. Armed with the analytical and communication skills of the liberal arts graduate, plus an understanding of government and how it works, the political science grad has much to offer. This is true both in the world of work and in that of master's and doctoral study.

So who is the ideal political science graduate? The person ready to seize the opportunities made possible by his or her studies in this field. Whether it means going on to advanced studies or entering the workforce, a major in political science can open many doors.

PART ONE

THE JOB SEARCH

CHAPTER ONE

THE SELF-ASSESSMENT

S elf-assessment is the process by which you begin to acknowledge your own particular blend of education, experiences, values, needs, and goals. It provides the foundation for career planning and the entire job search process. Self-assessment involves looking inward and asking yourself what can sometimes prove to be difficult questions. This self-examination should lead to an intimate understanding of your personal traits, your personal values, your consumption patterns and economic needs, your longer-term goals, your skill base, your preferred skills, and your under-developed skills.

You come to the self-assessment process knowing yourself well in some of these areas, but you may still be uncertain about other aspects. You may be well aware of your consumption patterns, but have you spent much time specifically identifying your longer-term goals or your personal values as they relate to work? No matter what level of self-assessment you have undertaken to date, it is now time to clarify all of these issues and questions as they relate to the job search.

The knowledge you gain in the self-assessment process will guide the rest of your job search. In this book, you will learn about all of the following tasks:

- Writing resumes

- Exploring possible job titles

- Identifying employment sites

- Networking

- Interviewing

- Following up

- Evaluating job offers

In each of these steps, you will rely on and return often to the understanding gained through your self-assessment. Any individual seeking employment must be able and willing to express these facets of his or her personality to recruiters and interviewers throughout the job search. This communication allows you to show the world who you are so that together with employers you can determine whether there will be a workable match with a given job or career path.

HOW TO CONDUCT A SELF-ASSESSMENT

The self-assessment process goes on naturally all the time. People ask you to clarify what you mean, or you make a purchasing decision, or you begin a new relationship. You react to the world and the world reacts to you. How you understand these interactions and any changes you might make because of them are part of the natural process of self-discovery. There is, however, a more comprehensive and efficient way to approach self-assessment with regard to employment.

Because self-assessment can become a complex exercise, we have distilled it into a seven-step process that provides an effective basis for undertaking a job search. The seven steps include the following:

1. Understanding your personal traits

2. Identifying your personal values

3. Calculating your economic needs

4. Exploring your longer-term goals

5. Enumerating your skill base

6. Recognizing your preferred skills

7. Assessing skills needing further development

As you work through your self-assessment, you might want to create a worksheet similar to the one shown in Exhibit 1.1. Or you might want to keep a journal of the thoughts you have as you undergo this process. There will be many opportunities to revise your self-assessment as you start down the path of seeking a career.

STEP 1   Understanding Your Personal Traits

Each person has a unique personality that he or she brings to the job search process. Gaining a better understanding of your personal traits can help you

Exhibit 1.1

Self-Assessment Worksheet

STEP 1. Understand Your Personal Traits
The personal traits that describe me are:
(Include all of the words that describe you.)

The ten personal traits that most accurately describe
me are: *(List these ten traits.)*

STEP 2. Identify Your Personal Values
Working conditions that are important to me include:
*(List working conditions that would have to exist for
you to accept a position.)*

The values that go along with my working conditions
are:
*(Write down the values that correspond to each
working condition.)*

Some additional values I've decided to include are:
*(List those values you identify as you conduct this job
search.)*

STEP 3. Calculate Your Economic Needs
My estimated minimum annual salary requirement is:
*(Write the salary you have calculated based on your
budget.)*

Starting salaries for the positions I'm considering are:
*(List the name of each job you are considering and
the associated starting salary.)*

STEP 4. Explore Your Longer-Term Goals
My thoughts on longer-term goals right now are:
*(Jot down some of your longer-term goals as you
know them right now.)*

continued

continued

STEP 5. Enumerate Your Skill Base

The general skills I possess are: *(List the skills that underlie tasks you are able to complete.)*

The specific skills I possess are:
(List more technical or specific skills that you possess and indicate your level of expertise.)

General and specific skills that I want to promote to employers for the jobs I'm considering are:
(List general and specific skills for each type of job you are considering.)

STEP 6. Recognize Your Preferred Skills

Skills that I would like to use on the job include:
(List skills that you hope to use on the job, and indicate how often you'd like to use them.)

STEP 7. Assess Skills Needing Further Development

Some skills that I'll need to acquire for the jobs I'm considering include:
(Write down skills listed in job advertisements or job descriptions that you don't currently possess.)

I believe I can build these skills by:
(Describe how you plan to acquire these skills.)

evaluate job and career choices. Identifying these traits, then finding employment that allows you to draw on at least some of them can create a rewarding and fulfilling work experience. If potential employment doesn't allow you to use these preferred traits, it is important to decide whether you can find other ways to express them or whether you would be better off not considering this type of job. Interests and hobbies pursued outside of work hours can be one way to use personal traits you don't have an opportunity to draw on in your work. For example, if you consider yourself an outgoing person and the kinds of jobs you are examining allow little contact with other people, you may be able to achieve the level of interaction that is comfortable for you outside of your work setting. If such a compromise seems impractical or otherwise unsatisfactory, you probably should explore only jobs that provide the interaction you want and need on the job.

Many young adults who are not very confident about their attractiveness to employers will downplay their need for income. They will say, "Money is not all that important if I love my work." But if you begin to document exactly what you need for housing, transportation, insurance, clothing, food, and utilities, you will begin to understand that some jobs cannot meet your financial needs and it doesn't matter how wonderful the job is. If you have to worry each payday about bills and other financial obligations, you won't be very effective on the job. Begin now to be honest with yourself about your needs.

Inventorying Your Personal Traits. Begin the self-assessment process by creating an inventory of your personal traits. Using the list in Exhibit 1.2, decide which of these personal traits describe you.

Exhibit 1.2		
Accurate	Cooperative	Flexible
Active	Courageous	Formal
Adaptable	Critical	Friendly
Adventurous	Curious	Future-oriented
Affectionate	Daring	Generous
Aggressive	Decisive	Gentle
Ambitious	Deliberate	Good-natured
Analytical	Detail-oriented	Helpful
Appreciative	Determined	Honest
Artistic	Discreet	Humorous
Brave	Dominant	Idealistic
Businesslike	Eager	Imaginative
Calm	Easygoing	Impersonal
Capable	Efficient	Independent
Caring	Emotional	Individualistic
Cautious	Empathetic	Industrious
Cheerful	Energetic	Informal
Clean	Excitable	Innovative
Competent	Expressive	Intellectual
Confident	Extroverted	Intelligent
Conscientious	Fair-minded	Introverted
Conservative	Farsighted	Intuitive
Considerate	Feeling	Inventive
Cool	Firm	Jovial

continued

continued

Just	Poised	Sensitive
Kind	Polite	Serious
Liberal	Practical	Sincere
Likable	Precise	Sociable
Logical	Principled	Spontaneous
Loyal	Private	Strong
Mature	Productive	Strong-minded
Methodical	Progressive	Structured
Meticulous	Quick	Subjective
Mistrustful	Quiet	Tactful
Modest	Rational	Thorough
Motivated	Realistic	Thoughtful
Objective	Receptive	Tolerant
Observant	Reflective	Trusting
Open-minded	Relaxed	Trustworthy
Opportunistic	Reliable	Truthful
Optimistic	Reserved	Understanding
Organized	Resourceful	Unexcitable
Original	Responsible	Uninhibited
Outgoing	Reverent	Verbal
Patient	Sedentary	Versatile
Peaceable	Self-confident	Wholesome
Personable	Self-controlled	Wise
Persuasive	Self-disciplined	
Pleasant	Sensible	

Focusing on Selected Personal Traits. Of all the traits you identified from the list in Exhibit 1.2, select the ten you believe most accurately describe you. If you are having a difficult time deciding, think about which words people who know you well would use to describe you. Keep track of these ten traits.

Considering Your Personal Traits in the Job Search Process. As you begin exploring jobs and careers, watch for matches between your personal traits and the job descriptions you read. Some jobs will require many personal traits you know you possess, and others will not seem to match those traits.

· ·

Working as a legislative assistant, for example, will draw upon your organizational, analytical, and communicative skills. You will need to gather and analyze information

from a variety of sources, and then summarize or explain important details. This might range from listening to a constituent's complaints and drafting a letter in response, to studying proposed legislation and recommending whether your employer should support it. You might not need the same level of public speaking abilities as a legislator, but the job will demand attention to detail and a good memory.

· ·

Your ability to respond to changing conditions, decision-making ability, productivity, creativity, and verbal skills all have a bearing on your success in and enjoyment of your work life. To better guarantee success, be sure to take the time needed to understand these traits in yourself.

STEP 2 Identifying Your Personal Values

Your personal values affect every aspect of your life, including employment, and they develop and change as you move through life. Values can be defined as principles that we hold in high regard, qualities that are important and desirable to us. Some values aren't ordinarily connected to work (love, beauty, color, light, marriage, family, or religion), and others are (autonomy, cooperation, effectiveness, achievement, knowledge, and security). Our values determine, in part, the level of satisfaction we feel in a particular job.

Defining Acceptable Working Conditions. One facet of employment is the set of working conditions that must exist for someone to consider taking a job.

Each of us would probably create a unique list of acceptable working conditions, but items that might be included on many people's lists are the amount of money you would need to be paid, how far you are willing to drive or travel, the amount of freedom you want in determining your own schedule, whether you would be working with people or data or things, and the types of tasks you would be willing to do. Your conditions might include statements of working conditions you will *not* accept; for example, you might not be willing to work at night or on weekends or holidays.

If you were offered a job tomorrow, what conditions would have to exist for you to realistically consider accepting the position? Take some time and make a list of these conditions.

Realizing Associated Values. Your list of working conditions can be used to create an inventory of your values relating to jobs and careers you are exploring. For example, if one of your conditions stated that you wanted to earn

---

Exhibit 1.3

Work Values

Achievement	Development	Physical activity
Advancement	Effectiveness	Power
Adventure	Excitement	Precision
Attainment	Fast pace	Prestige
Authority	Financial gain	Privacy
Autonomy	Helping	Profit
Belonging	Humor	Recognition
Challenge	Improvisation	Risk
Change	Independence	Security
Communication	Influencing others	Self-expression
Community	Intellectual stimulation	Solitude
Competition	Interaction	Stability
Completion	Knowledge	Status
Contribution	Leading	Structure
Control	Mastery	Supervision
Cooperation	Mobility	Surroundings
Creativity	Moral fulfillment	Time freedom
Decision making	Organization	Variety

---

at least $25,000 per year, the associated value would be financial gain. If another condition was that you wanted to work with a friendly group of people, the value that goes along with that might be belonging or interaction with people. Exhibit 1.3 provides a list of commonly held values that relate to the work environment; use it to create your own list of personal values.

Relating Your Values to the World of Work. As you read the job descriptions in this book and in other suggested resources, think about the values associated with each position.

· ·

For example, in working as a legislative assistant, your duties may include writing draft versions of speeches or reports, scheduling meetings for your employer, and talking on the telephone with constituents or potential voters.

· ·

If you were thinking about a career in this field, or any other field you're exploring, at least some of the associated values should match those you extracted from your list of working conditions. Take a second look at any values that don't match up. How important are they to you? What will happen if they are not satisfied on the job? Can you incorporate those personal values elsewhere? Your answers need to be brutally honest. As you continue your exploration, be sure to add to your list any additional values that occur to you.

STEP 3　Calculating Your Economic Needs

Each of us grew up in an environment that provided for certain basic needs, such as food and shelter, and, to varying degrees, other needs that we now consider basic, such as cable TV, reading materials, or an automobile. Needs such as privacy, space, and quiet, which at first glance may not appear to be monetary needs, may add to housing expenses and so should be considered as you examine your economic needs. For example, if you place a high value on a large, open living space for yourself, it would be difficult to satisfy that need without an associated high housing cost, especially in a densely populated city environment.

As you prepare to move into the world of work and become responsible for meeting your own basic needs, it is important to consider the salary you will need to be able to afford a satisfying standard of living. The three-step process outlined here will help you plan a budget, which in turn will allow you to evaluate the various career choices and geographic locations you are considering. The steps include (1) developing a realistic budget, (2) examining starting salaries, and (3) using a cost-of-living index.

Developing a Realistic Budget. Each of us has certain expectations for the kind of lifestyle we want to maintain. In order to begin the process of defining your economic needs, it will be helpful to determine what you expect to spend on routine monthly expenses. These expenses include housing, food, transportation, entertainment, utilities, loan repayments, and revolving charge accounts. A worksheet that details many of these expenses is shown in Exhibit 1.4. You may not currently spend for certain items, but you probably

---

Exhibit 1.4

Estimated Monthly Expenses Worksheet

		Could Reduce Spending? (Yes/No)
Cable	$ _____	_____
Child care	_____	_____

continued

continued

		Could Reduce Spending? (Yes/No)
Clothing	_____	_____
Educational loan repayment	_____	_____
Entertainment	_____	_____
Food	_____	_____
At home	_____	_____
Meals out	_____	_____
Gifts	_____	_____
Housing		
Rent/mortgage	_____	_____
Insurance	_____	_____
Property taxes	_____	_____
Medical insurance	_____	_____
Reading materials		
Newspapers	_____	_____
Magazines	_____	_____
Books	_____	_____
Revolving loans/charges	_____	_____
Savings	_____	_____
Telephone	_____	_____
Transportation		
Auto payment	_____	_____
Insurance	_____	_____
Parking	_____	_____
Gasoline	_____	_____
—or		
Cab/train/bus fare	_____	_____
Utilities		
Electric	_____	_____
Gas	_____	_____
Water/sewer	_____	_____
Vacations	_____	_____
Miscellaneous expense 1	_____	_____
Expense: _____		
Miscellaneous expense 2	_____	_____
Expense: _____		
Miscellaneous expense 3	_____	_____
Expense: _____		

TOTAL MONTHLY EXPENSES:_____

YEARLY EXPENSES (Monthly expenses x 12): _____

INCREASE TO INCLUDE TAXES (Yearly expenses x 1.35): ____ =

MINIMUM ANNUAL SALARY REQUIREMENT _____

will have to once you begin supporting yourself. As you develop this budget, be generous in your estimates, but keep in mind any items that could be reduced or eliminated. If you are not sure about the cost of a certain item, talk with family or friends who would be able to give you a realistic estimate.

If this is new or difficult for you, start to keep a log of expenses right now. You may be surprised at how much you actually spend each month for food or stamps or magazines. Household expenses and personal grooming items can often loom very large in a budget, as can auto repairs or home maintenance.

Income taxes must also be taken into consideration when examining salary requirements. State and local taxes vary by location, so it is difficult to calculate exactly the effect of taxes on the amount of income you need to generate. To roughly estimate the gross income necessary to generate your minimum annual salary requirement, multiply the minimum salary you have calculated (see Exhibit 1.4) by a factor of 1.35. The resulting figure will be an approximation of what your gross income would need to be, given your estimated expenses.

Examining Starting Salaries. Starting salaries for each of the career tracks are provided throughout this book. These salary figures can be used in conjunction with the cost-of-living index (discussed in the next section) to determine whether you would be able to meet your basic economic needs in a given geographic location.

Using a Cost-of-Living Index. If you are thinking about trying to get a job in a geographic region other than the one where you now live, understanding differences in the cost of living will help you come to a more informed decision about making a move. By using a cost-of-living index, you can compare salaries offered and the cost of living in different locations with what you know about the salaries offered and the cost of living in your present location.

Many variables are used to calculate the cost-of-living index, including housing expenses, groceries, utilities, transportation, health care, clothing, entertainment, local income taxes, and local sales taxes. Cost-of-living indices can be found in many resources, such as *Equal Employment Opportunity Bimonthly*, *Places Rated Almanac*, or *The Best Towns in America*. They are constantly being recalculated based on changes in costs.

··

If you lived in Cleveland, Ohio, for example, and you were interested in working as a high school political science teacher, you would earn, on average, $37,835 annually. But let's say you're thinking about moving to either

New York, Los Angeles, or Denver. You know you can live on $37,835 in Cleveland, but you want to be able to equal that salary in other locations you're considering. How much will you need to earn in those locations to do this? Figuring the cost of living for each city will show you.

Let's walk through this example. In any cost-of-living index, the number 100 represents the national average cost of living, and each city is assigned an index number based on current prices in that city for the items included in the index (housing, food, etc.). In the index we used, New York was assigned the number 213.3, Los Angeles' index was 124.6, Denver's was 100.0, and Cleveland's index was 114.3. In other words, it costs more than twice as much to live in New York as it does in Denver. We can set up a table to determine exactly how much you would have to earn in each of these cities to have the same buying power that you have in Cleveland.

Job: High school political science teacher

CITY	INDEX	EQUIVALENT SALARY

$$\frac{\text{New York}}{\text{Cleveland}} \quad \frac{213.3}{114.3} \times \$37{,}835 = \$70{,}605 \text{ in New York}$$

$$\frac{\text{Los Angeles}}{\text{Cleveland}} \quad \frac{124.6}{114.3} \times \$37{,}835 = \$41{,}244 \text{ in Los Angeles}$$

$$\frac{\text{Denver}}{\text{Cleveland}} \quad \frac{100.0}{114.3} \times \$37{,}835 = \$33{,}101 \text{ in Denver}$$

You would have to earn $70,605 in New York, $41,244 in Los Angeles, and $33,101 in Denver to match the buying power of $37,835 in Cleveland.

If you would like to determine whether it's financially worthwhile to make any of these moves, one more piece of information is needed: the salaries of high school political science teachers in these other cities. The *American Salaries and Wages Survey* (4th edition) reports the following average salary information for high school social science teachers (which includes political science teachers).

	Annual Salary	Salary Equivalent to Ohio	Change in Buying Power
New York	$48,115	$70,605	−$22,490
Los Angeles	$43,114	$41,244	+$ 1,870
Denver	$35,364	$33,101	+$ 2,263
Cleveland	$37,835	—	—

If you moved to New York City and secured employment as a high school political science teacher, you would not be able to maintain a lifestyle similar to the one you led in Cleveland; in fact, you would have to add almost 50 percent to your income to maintain a similar lifestyle in New York. The same would not be true for a move to Los Angeles or Denver. You would increase your buying power given the rate of pay and cost of living in these cities.

••

You can work through a similar exercise for any type of job you are considering and for many locations when current salary information is available. It will be worth your time to undertake this analysis if you are seriously considering a relocation. By doing so you will be able to make an informed choice.

STEP 4 Exploring Your Longer-Term Goals

There is no question that when we first begin working, our goals are to use our skills and education in a job that will reward us with employment, income, and status relative to the preparation we brought with us to this position. If we are not being paid as much as we feel we should for our level of education, or if job demands don't provide the intellectual stimulation we had hoped for, we experience unhappiness and as a result often seek other employment.

Most jobs we consider "good" are those that fulfill our basic "lower-level" needs of security, food, clothing, shelter, income, and productive work. But even when our basic needs are met and our jobs are secure and productive, we as individuals are constantly changing. As we change, the demands and expectations we place on our jobs may change. Fortunately, some jobs grow and change with us, and this explains why some people are happy through-out many years in a job.

But more often people are bigger than the jobs they fill. We have more goals and needs than any job could fulfill. These are "higher-level" needs of self-esteem, companionship, affection, and an increasing desire to feel we are employing ourselves in the most effective way possible. Not all of these higher-level needs can be fulfilled through employment, but for as long as we are employed, we increasingly demand that our jobs play their part in moving us along the path to fulfillment.

Another obvious but important fact is that we change as we mature. Although our jobs also have the potential for change, they may not change as frequently or as markedly as we do. There are increasingly fewer one-job, one-employer careers; we must think about a work future that may involve voluntary or forced moves from employer to employer. Because of that very real possibility, we need to take advantage of the opportunities in each position we hold to acquire skills and competencies that will keep us viable and attractive as employees in a job market that is not only increasingly technology/computer dependent, but also is populated with more and more small, self-transforming organizations rather than the large, seemingly stable organizations of the past.

It may be difficult in the early stages of the job search to determine whether the path you are considering can meet these longer-term goals. Reading about career paths and individual career histories in your field can be very helpful in this regard. Meeting and talking with individuals further along in their careers can be enlightening as well. Older workers can provide valuable guidance on "self-managing" your career, which will become an increasingly valuable skill in the future. Some of these ideas may seem remote as you read this now, but you should be able to appreciate the need to ensure that you are growing, developing valuable new skills, and researching other employers who might be interested in your particular skills package.

· ·

If you are considering a position as an urban planner, you would gain a better perspective on this career if you could talk to an entry-level planning assistant, a more senior and experienced town planner or city planner, and finally, a director of planning for a city, town, or county who has had a considerable work history in urban planning. Each will have a different perspective, unique concerns, and an individual set of value priorities.

· ·

STEP 5   Enumerating Your Skill Base

In terms of the job search, skills can be thought of as capabilities that can be developed in school, at work, or by volunteering and then used in specific job settings. Many studies have documented the kinds of skills that employers seek in entry-level applicants. For example, some of the most desired skills for individuals interested in the teaching profession include the ability to interact effectively with students one on one, to manage a classroom, to adapt to varying situations as necessary, and to get involved in school activities. Business employers have also identified important qualities, including enthusiasm for the employer's product or service, a businesslike mind, the ability to follow written or verbal instructions, the ability to demonstrate self-control, the confidence to suggest new ideas, the ability to communicate with all members of a group, awareness of cultural differences, and loyalty, to name just a few. You will find that many of these skills are also in the repertoire of qualities demanded in your college major.

In order to be successful in obtaining any given job, you must be able to demonstrate that you possess a certain mix of skills that will allow you to carry out the duties required by that job. This skill mix will vary a great deal from job to job; to determine the skills necessary for the jobs you are seeking, you can read job advertisements or more generic job descriptions, such as those found later in this book. If you want to be effective in the job search, you must directly show employers that you possess the skills needed to be successful in filling the position. These skills will initially be described on your resume and then discussed again during the interview process.

Skills are either general or specific. General skills are those that are developed throughout the college years by taking classes, being employed, and getting involved in other related activities such as volunteer work or campus organizations. General skills include the ability to read and write, to perform computations, to think critically, and to communicate effectively. Specific skills are also acquired on the job and in the classroom, but they allow you to complete tasks that require specialized knowledge. Computer programming, drafting, language translating, and copyediting are just a few examples of specific skills that may relate to a given job.

In order to develop a list of skills relevant to employers, you must first identify the general skills you possess, then list specific skills you have to offer, and, finally, examine which of these skills employers are seeking.

Identifying Your General Skills. Because you possess or will possess a college degree, employers will assume that you can read and write, perform certain basic computations, think critically, and communicate effectively. Employers will want to see that you have acquired these skills, and they will want to know which additional general skills you possess.

One way to begin identifying skills is to write an experiential diary. An experiential diary lists all the tasks you were responsible for completing for each job you've held and then outlines the skills required to do those tasks. You may list several skills for any given task. This diary allows you to distinguish between the tasks you performed and the underlying skills required to complete those tasks. Here's an example:

Tasks	Skills
Answering telephone	Effective use of language, clear diction, ability to direct inquiries, ability to solve problems
Waiting on tables	Poise under conditions of time and pressure, speed, accuracy, good memory, simultaneous completion of tasks, sales skills

For each job or experience you have participated in, develop a worksheet based on the example shown here. On a resume, you may want to describe these skills rather than simply listing tasks. Skills are easier for the employer to appreciate, especially when your experience is very different from the employment you are seeking. In addition to helping you identify general skills, this experiential diary will prepare you to speak more effectively in an interview about the qualifications you possess.

Identifying Your Specific Skills. It may be easier to identify your specific skills because you can definitely say whether you can speak other languages, program a computer, draft a map or diagram, or edit a document using appropriate symbols and terminology.

Using your experiential diary, identify the points in your history where you learned how to do something very specific, and decide whether you have a beginning, intermediate, or advanced knowledge of how to use that particular skill. Right now, be sure to list *every* specific skill you have, and don't consider whether you like using the skill. Write down a list of specific skills you have acquired and the level of competence you possess—beginning, intermediate, or advanced.

Relating Your Skills to Employers. You probably have thought about a couple of different jobs you might be interested in obtaining, and one way to begin relating the general and specific skills you possess to a potential employer's needs is to read actual advertisements for these types of positions (see Part II for resources listing actual job openings).

. . . .

For example, you might be interested in working as an economic analyst for a government agency that deals with foreign trade, prior to returning to graduate school to seek a master's degree in international relations with a specialty in economics. A typical job listing might read "conduct trade policy analysis, economic evaluations, and import-export studies. Bachelor's degree in economics, international business, or political science required. International experience preferred." If you then used any one of a number of sources of information that described the job of policy analyst or international trade specialist, you would find additional information. Policy analysts in this area track and report on trade laws and policies, interpret laws and regulations, and advise senior managers about economic and political policies.

Begin building a comprehensive list of required skills with the first job description you read. Exploring advertisements for several types of related positions will reveal an important core of skills necessary for obtaining the type of work you're interested in. Include both general and specific skills.

Following is a sample list of skills needed to be successful as a policy analyst in international trade.

Job: International trade policy analyst	
General Skills	**Specific Skills**
Accounting	Estimate trade volume
Reading	Track development of foreign legislation related to trade
Gathering information	Compile trade figures
Decision making	Evaluate alternatives
Meeting deadlines	Prepare reports
Attending meetings	Communicating recommendations for policy changes
Entering data into computer	Preparing quarterly trade summaries
Writing	Edit trade reports

On separate sheets of paper, try to generate a list of required skills for at least one job you are considering.

The list of general skills that you develop for a given career path would be valuable for any number of jobs you

might seek. Many specific skills would also be transferable to other types of positions. For example, editing reports is a required skill for other types of analysts and for almost any management position. The ability to use basic word processing and spreadsheet software would also be useful in almost any job setting.

••

Now review the list of skills you developed and check off those skills that *you know you possess* and that are required for jobs you are considering. You should refer to these specific skills on the resume that you write for this type of job. See Chapter 2 for details on resume writing.

STEP 6 Recognizing Your Preferred Skills

In the previous section you developed a comprehensive list of skills that relate to particular career paths that are of interest to you. You can now relate these to skills that you prefer to use. We all use a wide range of skills (some researchers say individuals have a repertoire of about 500 skills), but we may not be particularly interested in using all of them in our work. There may be some skills that come to us more naturally or that we use successfully time and time again and that we want to continue to use; these are best described as our preferred skills. For this exercise use the list of skills that you developed for the previous section and decide which of them you are *most interested in using* in future work and how often you would like to use them. You might be interested in using some skills only occasionally, while others you would like to use more regularly. You probably also have skills that you hope you can use constantly.

As you examine job announcements, look for matches between this list of preferred skills and the qualifications described in the advertisements. These skills should be highlighted on your resume and discussed in job interviews.

STEP 7 Assessing Skills Needing Further Development

Previously you developed a list of general and specific skills required for given positions. You already possess some of these skills; those that remain to be developed are your underdeveloped skills.

If you are just beginning the job search, there may be gaps between the qualifications required for some of the jobs being considered and skills you possess. These are your underdeveloped skills. The thought of having to admit to and talk about these underdeveloped skills, especially in a job interview, is a frightening one. One way to put a healthy perspective on this subject is to target and relate your exploration of underdeveloped skills to the types of positions you are seeking. Recognizing these shortcomings and planning to overcome them with either on-the-job training or additional formal education can be a positive way to address the concept of underdeveloped skills.

On your worksheet or in your journal, make a list of up to five general or specific skills required for the positions you're interested in that you *don't currently possess.* For each item list an idea you have for specific action you could take to acquire that skill. Do some brainstorming to come up with possible actions. If you have a hard time generating ideas, talk to people currently working in this type of position, professionals in your college career services office, trusted friends, family members, or members of related professional associations.

If, for example, you are interested in a job for which you don't have some specific required experience, you could locate training opportunities such as classes or workshops offered through a local college or university, community college, or club or association that would help you build the level of expertise you need for the job.

Many excellent jobs in today's economy demand computer skills you probably already have. Most graduates are not so lucky and have to acquire these skills—often before an employer will give their application serious consideration. So, what can you do if you find there are certain skills you're missing? If you're still in school, try to fill the gaps in your knowledge before you graduate. If you've already graduated, look at evening programs, continuing education courses, or tutorial programs that may be available commercially. Developing a modest level of expertise will encourage you to be more confident in suggesting to potential employers that you can continue to add to your skill base on the job.

In Chapter 5 on interviewing we will discuss in detail how to effectively address questions about underdeveloped skills. Generally speaking, though, employers want genuine answers to these types of questions. They want you to reveal "the real you," and they also want to see how you answer difficult questions. In taking the positive, targeted approach discussed above, you show the employer that you are willing to continue to learn and that you have a plan for strengthening your job qualifications.

USING YOUR SELF-ASSESSMENT

Exploring entry-level career options can be an exciting experience if you have good resources available and will take the time to use them. Can you effectively complete the following tasks?

1. Understand and relate your personality traits to career choices.

2. Define your personal values.

3. Determine your economic needs.

4. Explore longer-term goals.

5. Understand your skill base.

6. Recognize your preferred skills.

7. Express a willingness to improve on your underdeveloped skills.

If so, then you can more meaningfully participate in the job search process by writing a more effective resume, finding job titles that represent work you are interested in doing, locating job sites that will provide the opportunity for you to use your strengths and skills, networking in an informed way, participating in focused interviews, getting the most out of follow-up contacts, and evaluating job offers to find those that create a good match between you and the employer.

The remaining chapters guide you through these next steps in the job search process. For many job seekers, this process can take anywhere from three months to a year to implement. The time you will need to put into your job search will depend on the type of job you want and the geographic location where you'd like to work. Think of your effort as a job in itself, requiring you to set aside time each, week to complete the needed work. Carefully undertaken efforts may reduce the time you need for your job search.

CHAPTER TWO

THE RESUME AND COVER LETTER

T he task of writing a resume may seem overwhelming if you are unfamiliar with this type of document, but there are some easily understood techniques that can and should be used. This section was written to help you understand the purpose of the resume, the different types of resume formats available, and how to write the sections of information traditionally found on a resume. We will present examples and explanations that address questions frequently posed by people writing their first resume or updating an old resume.

Even within the formats and suggestions given below, however, there are infinite variations. True, most resumes follow one of the outlines suggested below, but you should feel free to adjust the resume to suit your needs and make it expressive of your life and experience.

WHY WRITE A RESUME?

The purpose of a resume is to convince an employer that you should be interviewed. You'll want to present enough information to show that you can make an immediate and valuable contribution to an organization. A resume is not an in-depth historical or legal document; later in the job search process you'll be asked to document your entire work history on an application form and attest to its validity. The resume should, instead, highlight relevant information pertaining directly to the organization that will receive the document or the type of position you are seeking.

We will discuss four types of resumes in this chapter: chronological resume, functional resume, targeted resume, and the broadcast letter. The reasons for using one type of resume over another and the typical format for each are addressed in the following sections.

THE CHRONOLOGICAL RESUME

The chronological resume is the most common of the various resume formats and therefore the format that employers are most used to receiving. This type of resume is easy to read and understand because it details the chronological progression of jobs you have held. (See Exhibit 2.1.) It begins with your most recent employment and works back in time. If you have a solid work history or have experience that provided growth and development in your duties and responsibilities, a chronological resume will highlight these achievements. The typical elements of a chronological resume include the heading, a career objective, educational background, employment experience, activities, and references.

The Heading
The heading consists of your name, address, and telephone number. Recently it has come to include fax numbers and electronic mail addresses as well. We suggest that you spell out your full name and type it in all capital letters in bold type. After all, you are the focus of the resume! If you have a current as well as a permanent address and you include both in the heading, be sure to indicate until what date your current address will be valid. Don't forget to include the zip code with your address and the area code with your telephone number.

The Objective
As you formulate the wording for this part of your resume, keep the following points in mind.

The Objective Focuses the Resume. Without a doubt this is the most challenging part of the resume for most resume writers. Even for individuals who have quite firmly decided on a career path, it can be difficult to encapsulate all they want to say in one or two brief sentences. For job seekers who are unfocused or unclear about their intentions, trying to write this section can inhibit the entire resume writing process.

Recruiters tell us, time and again, that the objective creates a frame of reference for them. It helps them see how you express your goals and career

Exhibit 2.1

Chronological Resume

JENNY VAN HORN

Apartment 234
Appleton Way Village
Marietta, GA 30061
(770) 555-1858

OBJECTIVE

Position teaching Civics or American Government. Interested in high school or middle school setting.

EDUCATION

Bachelor of Science, University of Georgia
Athens, Georgia, May 1998
Major: Political Education
Minor: Teacher Education

Honors/Activities: Vice President of Student Government
   Association
President, Political Science Club
Member, Student Ambassadors
Dean's List four semesters, President's List
   three semesters
Recipient, John Waggens Award (outstanding
   political science student)
Magna cum laude graduate

EXPERIENCE

Peer Tutor, University of Georgia Academic Support Center,
   1996–97
Provided tutoring in a variety of subjects for freshmen
   experiencing academic difficulty
Youth Counselor, Trinity United Methodist Church, Dublin,
   Georgia, 1995–98
Assisted youth minister in planning youth activities, conducting
   weekly sessions, and providing oversight during retreats and
   other activities

continued

---

continued

Intern, Georgia Political Action Center, Summer 1995
Assisted in compiling election data and completing reports
    regarding voter preferences in 1994 elections

COMMUNITY SERVICE

Active volunteer with church activities; election day poll worker;
Habitat for Humanity volunteer

REFERENCES

A selection of both personal and professional references will be
provided on request.

---

focus. In addition, the statement may indicate in what ways you can immediately benefit an organization. Given the importance of the objective, every
point covered in the resume should relate to it. If information doesn't relate,
it should be omitted. With the word processing technology available today,
each resume can and should be tailored for individual employers or specific
positions that are available.

Choose an Appropriate Length. Because of the brevity necessary for a resume,
you should keep the objective as short as possible. Although objectives of only
four or five words often don't show much direction, objectives that take three
full lines would be viewed as too wordy and might possibly be ignored.

Consider Which Type of Objective Statement You Will Use. There are many ways
to state an objective, but generally there are four forms this statement can
take: (1) a very general statement; (2) a statement focused on a specific position; (3) a statement focused on a specific industry; or (4) a summary of your
qualifications. In our contacts with employers, we often hear that many
resumes don't exhibit any direction or career goals, so we suggest avoiding
general statements when possible.

1. General Objective Statement. General objective statements look like the
following:

- An entry-level educational programming coordinator position
- An entry-level marketing position

This type of objective would be useful if you know what type of job you
want but you're not sure which industries interest you.

2. Position-Focused Objective. Following are examples of objectives focusing on a specific position:

- ❑ To obtain the position of director of public information at the State Council for Environmental Quality
- ❑ To obtain a position as assistant town manager

When a student applies for an advertised job opening, this type of focus can be very effective. The employer knows that the applicant has taken the time to tailor the resume specifically for this position.

3. Industry-Focused Objective. Focusing on a particular industry in an objective could be stated as follows:

- ❑ To begin a career as a sales representative in the cruise line industry

4. Summary of Qualifications Statement. The summary of qualifications can be used instead of an objective or in conjunction with an objective. The purpose of this type of statement is to highlight relevant qualifications gained through a variety of experiences. This type of statement is often used by individuals with extensive and diversified work experience. An example of a qualifications statement follows:

··

A degree in political science and four years of progressively increasing job responsibility in a regional planning agency have prepared me to begin a career as a manager in a government agency where thoroughness and attention to detail are valued.

··

Support Your Objective. A resume that contains any one of these types of objective statements should then go on to demonstrate why you are qualified to get the position. Listing academic degrees can be one way to indicate qualifications. Another demonstration would be in the way previous experiences, both volunteer and paid, are described. Without this kind of documentation in the body of the resume, the objective looks unsupported. Think of the resume as telling a connected story about you. All the elements should work together to form a coherent picture that ideally should relate to your statement of objective.

Education

This section of your resume should indicate the exact name of the degree you will receive or have received, spelled out completely with no abbreviations. The degree is generally listed after the objective, followed by the institution name and address, and then the month and year of graduation. This section could also include your academic minor, grade point average (GPA), and appearance on the Dean's List or President's List.

If you have enough space, you might want to include a section listing courses related to the field in which you are seeking work. The best use of a "related courses" section would be to list some course work that is not traditionally associated with the major. Perhaps you took several computer courses outside your degree that will be helpful and related to the job prospects you are entertaining. Several education section examples are shown here:

• •

❑ **Bachelor of Science Degree in Political Science**
   State University, Boulder, Colorado, 1998
   Concentration: American Governmental Systems

❑ **Bachelor of Science Degree with Major in**
      Political Science
   University of South Carolina, Columbia, SC,
      May 1998
   Minor: U.S. History

❑ **Bachelor of Arts Degree in Political Science**
   West Virginia State College, Institute, West
      Virginia, 1998
   General Political Science option
   Minor in History

An example of a format for a related course section follows:

RELATED COURSES	
American Government	Judicial Systems
Constitutional Law	Legislative Processes
State and Local Government	Advanced Seminar: The Electoral Process

• •

Experience

The experience section of your resume should be the most substantial part and should take up most of the space on the page. Employers want to see what kind of work history you have. They will look at your range of experiences, longevity in jobs, and specific tasks you are able to complete. This section may also be called "work experience," "related experience," "employment history," or "employment." No matter what you call this section, some important points to remember are the following:

1. **Describe your duties** as they relate to the position you are seeking.

2. **Emphasize major responsibilities** and indicate increases in responsibility. Include all relevant employment experiences: summer, part-time, internships, cooperative education, or self-employment.

3. **Emphasize skills,** especially those that transfer from one situation to another. The fact that you coordinated a student organization, chaired meetings, supervised others, and managed a budget leads one to suspect that you could coordinate other things as well.

4. **Use descriptive job titles** that provide information about what you did. A "Student Intern" should be more specifically stated as, for example, "Magazine Operations Intern." "Volunteer" is also too general; a title like "Peer Writing Tutor" would be more appropriate.

5. **Create word pictures** by using active verbs to start sentences. Describe *results* you have produced in the work you have done.

A limp description would say something like the following: "My duties included helping with production, proofreading, and editing. I used a word processing package to alter text." An action statement would be stated as follows: "Coordinated and assisted in the creative marketing of brochures and seminar promotions, becoming proficient in WordPerfect."

Remember, an accomplishment is simply a result, a final measurable product that people can relate to. A duty is not a result, it is an obligation—every job holder has duties. For an effective resume, list as many results as you can. To make the most of the limited space you have and to give your description impact, carefully select appropriate and accurate descriptors from the list of action words in Exhibit 2.2.

Here are some traits that employers tell us they like to see:

- Teamwork
- Energy and motivation
- Learning and using new skills
- Demonstrated versatility

Exhibit 2.2

Resume Action Verbs

Achieved	Established	Operated
Acted	Estimated	Organized
Administered	Evaluated	Participated
Advised	Examined	Performed
Analyzed	Explained	Planned
Assessed	Facilitated	Predicted
Assisted	Finalized	Prepared
Attained	Generated	Presented
Balanced	Handled	Processed
Budgeted	Headed	Produced
Calculated	Helped	Projected
Collected	Identified	Proposed
Communicated	Illustrated	Provided
Compiled	Implemented	Qualified
Completed	Improved	Quantified
Composed	Increased	Questioned
Conceptualized	Influenced	Realized
Condensed	Informed	Received
Conducted	Initiated	Recommended
Consolidated	Innovated	Recorded
Constructed	Instituted	Reduced
Controlled	Instructed	Reinforced
Converted	Integrated	Reported
Coordinated	Interpreted	Represented
Corrected	Introduced	Researched
Created	Learned	Resolved
Decreased	Lectured	Reviewed
Defined	Led	Scheduled
Demonstrated	Maintained	Selected
Designed	Managed	Served
Determined	Mapped	Showed
Developed	Marketed	Simplified
Directed	Met	Sketched
Documented	Modified	Sold
Drafted	Monitored	Solved
Edited	Negotiated	Staffed
Eliminated	Observed	Streamlined
Ensured	Obtained	Studied

continued

continued		
Submitted	Tabulated	Updated
Summarized	Tested	Verified
Systematized	Transacted	

- Critical thinking

- Understanding how profits are created

- Displaying organizational acumen

- Communicating directly and clearly, in both writing and speaking

- Risk taking

- Willingness to admit mistakes

- Manifesting high personal standards

SOLUTIONS TO FREQUENTLY ENCOUNTERED PROBLEMS

Repetitive Employment with the Same Employer

EMPLOYMENT: The Foot Locker, Portland, Oregon. Summer 1991, 1992, 1993. Initially employed in high school as salesclerk. Due to successful performance, asked to return next two summers at higher pay with added responsibility. Ranked as the #2 salesperson the first summer and #1 the next two summers. Assisted in arranging eye-catching retail displays; served as manager of other summer workers during owner's absence.

A Large Number of Jobs

EMPLOYMENT: Recent Hospitality Industry Experience: Affiliated with four upscale hotel/restaurant complexes (September 1991–February 1994), where I worked part- and full-time as a waiter, bartender, disc jockey, and bookkeeper to produce income for college.

Several Positions with the Same Employer

EMPLOYMENT: Coca-Cola Bottling Co., Burlington, VT, 1991–94. In four years, I received three promotions, each with increased pay and responsibility.

Summer Sales Coordinator: Promoted to hire, train, and direct efforts of add-on staff of 15 college-age route salespeople hired to meet summer peak demand for product.

Sales Administrator: Promoted to run home office sales desk, managing accounts and associated delivery schedules for professional sales force of ten people. Intensive phone work, daily interaction with all personnel, and strong knowledge of product line required.

Route Salesperson: Summer employment to travel and tourism industry sites using Coke products. Met specific schedule demands, used good communication skills with wide variety of customers, and demonstrated strong selling skills. Named salesperson of the month for July and August of that year.

QUESTIONS RESUME WRITERS OFTEN ASK

How Far Back Should I Go in Terms of Listing Past Jobs?
Usually, listing three or four jobs should suffice. If you did something back in high school that has a bearing on your future aspirations for employment, by all means list the job. As you progress through your college career, high school jobs may be replaced on the resume by college employment.

Should I Differentiate Between Paid and Nonpaid Employment?
Most employers are not initially concerned about how much you were paid. They are anxious to know how much responsibility you held in your past employment. There is no need to specify that your work was volunteer if you had significant responsibilities.

How Should I Represent My Accomplishments or Work-Related Responsibilities?
Succinctly, but fully. In other words, give the employer enough information to arouse curiosity, but not so much detail that you leave nothing to the imagination. Besides, some jobs merit more lengthy explanations than others. Be sure to convey any information that can give an employer a better understanding of the depth of your involvement at work. Did you supervise others? How many? Did your efforts result in a more efficient operation? How much did you increase efficiency? Did you handle a budget? How much? Were you promoted in a short time? Did you work two jobs at once or 15 hours per week after high school? Where appropriate, quantify.

Should the Work Section Always Follow the Education Section on the Resume?

Always lead with your strengths. If your education closely relates to the employment you now seek, put this section after the objective. Or, if you are weak on the academic side but have a surplus of good work experiences, consider reversing the order of your sections to lead with employment, followed by education.

How Should I Present My Activities, Honors, Awards, Professional Societies, and Affiliations?

This section of the resume can add valuable information for an employer to consider if used correctly. The rule of thumb for information in this section is to include only those activities that are in some way relevant to the objective stated on your resume. If you can draw a valid connection between your activities and your objective, include them; if not, leave them out.

Granted, this is hard to do. Playing center on the championship basketball team or serving as coordinator of the biggest homecoming parade ever held are roles that have meaning for you and represent personal accomplishments you'd like to share. But the resume is a brief document, and the information you provide on it should help the employer make a decision about your job eligibility. Including personal details can be confusing and could hurt your candidacy. Limiting your activity list to a few very significant experiences can be very effective.

If you are applying for a position as a safety officer, your certificate in Red Cross lifesaving skills or CPR would be related and valuable. You would want to include it. If, however, you are applying for a job as a junior account executive in an advertising agency, that information would be unrelated and superfluous. Leave it out.

Professional affiliations and honors should *all* be listed; especially important are those related to your job objective. Social clubs and activities need not be a part of your resume unless you hold a significant office or you are looking for a position related to your membership. Be aware that most prospective employers' principle concerns are related to your employability, not your social life. If you have any, publications can be included as an addendum to your resume.

The focus of the resume is your experience and education. It is not necessary to describe your involvement in activities. However, if your resume needs to be lengthened, this section provides the freedom either to expand on or mention only briefly the contributions you have made. If you have made significant contributions (e.g., an officer of an organization or a particularly long tenure with a group), you may choose to describe them in more detail.

It is not always necessary to include the dates of your memberships with your activities the way you would include job dates.

There are a number of different ways in which to present additional information. You may give this section a number of different titles. Assess what you want to list, and then use an appropriate title. Do not use extracurricular activities. This terminology is scholastic, not professional, and therefore not appropriate. The following are two examples:

❑ ACTIVITIES: Society for Technical Communication, Student Senate, Student Admissions Representative, Senior Class Officer

❑ ACTIVITIES:
  • Society for Technical Communication Member
  • Student Senator
  • Student Admissions Representative
  • Senior Class Officer

The position you are looking for will determine what you should or should not include. *Always* look for a correlation between the activity and the prospective job.

How Should I Handle References?

The use of references is considered a part of the interview process, and they should never be listed on a resume. You would always provide references to a potential employer if requested to, so it is not even necessary to include this section on the resume if room does not permit. If space is available, it is acceptable to include one of the following statements:

❑ REFERENCES: Furnished upon request.

❑ REFERENCES: Available upon request.

Individuals used as references must be protected from unnecessary contacts. By including names on your resume, you leave your references unprotected. Overuse and abuse of your references will lead to less-than-supportive comments. Protect your references by giving out their names only when you are being considered seriously as a candidate for a given position.

THE FUNCTIONAL RESUME

The functional resume departs from a chronological resume in that it organizes information by specific accomplishments in various settings: previous

Exhibit 2.3

Functional Resume

ROBERT A. WATSON
126 Darst Avenue
Austin, TX 78767
(512) 555-0233 (voice)
(512) 555-1888 (fax)

OBJECTIVE
An entry-level position in public service, international affairs, or a related area. Special interest in public relations/public affairs.

CAPABILITIES
- Energetic and task-oriented
- Excellent quantitative and analytical skills
- Fluent in Spanish
- Interested and well-informed in international affairs
- Highly skilled in written and oral communications
- Adept in use of computers
- Experienced international traveler

SELECTED ACCOMPLISHMENTS
POLITICAL ACTIVITY: Two years of experience as volunteer campaign worker for Senator Alberto Sanchez. Assisted in developing campaign literature. Manned phone banks. Assisted in scheduling campaign activities.
WRITING/EDITING: Extensive experience in writing newsletters, brochures, and news releases. Familiar with Associated Press style requirements. Skilled in use of WordPerfect and other word processing software. Have had some experience in layout and design.
LEADERSHIP: President, University of Texas Young Democrats Association. Vice-chairman, Students for the Environment. Eagle Scout.

AWARDS
Lyndon Johnson Award, University of Texas Student Government Association, 1997
Outstanding Young Man of America, 1998

continued

---

continued

EMPLOYMENT HISTORY
Intern, Texas Trade Authority, Summer 1997
Telemarketer, Amsats Incorporated, Austin, Texas, Summer 1995
   and 1996

EDUCATION
Bachelor of Arts, University of Texas, 1998
Major: Political Science
Minor: Economics

REFERENCES
Available on request.

---

jobs, volunteer work, associations, etc. This type of resume permits you to stress the substance of your experiences rather than the position titles you have held. (See Exhibit 2.3.) You should consider using a functional resume if you have held a series of similar jobs that relied on the same skills or abilities.

The Objective

A functional resume begins with an objective that can be used to focus the contents of the resume.

Specific Accomplishments

Specific accomplishments are listed on this type of resume. Examples of the types of headings used to describe these capabilities might include sales, counseling, teaching, communication, production, management, marketing, or writing. The headings you choose will directly relate to your experience and the tasks that you carried out. Each accomplishment section contains statements related to your experience in that category, regardless of when or where it occurred. Organize the accomplishments and the related tasks you describe in their order of importance as related to the position you seek.

Experience or Employment History

Your actual work experience is condensed and placed after the specific accomplishments section. It simply lists dates of employment, position titles, and employer names.

Education

The education section of a functional resume is identical to that of the chronological resume, but it does not carry the same visual importance because it is placed near the bottom of the page.

References

Because actual reference names are never listed on a resume, this section is optional if space does not permit.

THE TARGETED RESUME

The targeted resume focuses on specific work-related capabilities you can bring to a given position within an organization. (See Exhibit 2.4.) It should be sent to an individual within the organization who makes hiring decisions about the position you are seeking.

The Objective

The objective on this type of resume should be targeted to a specific career or position. It should be supported by the capabilities, accomplishments, and achievements documented in the resume.

Exhibit 2.4

Targeted Resume

JACOB BURNHAM

22 Monument House
Cleveland, OH 44114
(216) 555-3498
(until May, 1998)

265 Weston Street
Columbus, OH 43229
(614) 888-4567

JOB TARGET
An entry-level position in nonprofit management or grant proposal development

CAPABILITIES
- Excellent writer and speaker
- Experienced in proposal development

continued

---

continued
- Proven team skills
- Familiar with a variety of computer software, including word processing software and spreadsheets

ACHIEVEMENTS
- Wrote winning proposal in student grant-writing contest
- Created student team to assist local youth in understanding electoral process
- Published my own newsletter on campus volunteerism

WORK HISTORY
Summer, 1997. Served internship with Cleveland Community Foundation, Cleveland, Ohio. Assisted in assembling grant proposals for review by foundation staff. Provided general office support.
1995–97. Student Assistant, Department of Political Science, Case Western Reserve University, Cleveland, Ohio. Assisted department chairperson in general office duties. Also conducted background research for grant-funded project on voting practices in 19th-century America.

EDUCATION
Earned Bachelor of Arts in Political Science
Case Western Reserve University

REFERENCES ON REQUEST

Capabilities

Capabilities should be statements that illustrate tasks you believe you are capable of based on your accomplishments, achievements, and work history. Each should relate to your targeted career or position. You can stress your qualifications rather than your employment history. This approach may require research to obtain an understanding of the nature of the work involved and the capabilities necessary to carry out that work.

Accomplishments/Achievements

This section relates the various activities you have been involved in to the job market. These experiences may include previous jobs, extracurricular activities at school, internships, and part-time summer work.

Experience

Your work history should be listed in abbreviated form and may include position title, employer name, and employment dates.

Education

Because this type of resume is directed toward a specific job target and an individual's related experience, the education section is not prominently located at the top of the resume as is done on the chronological resume.

THE BROADCAST LETTER

The broadcast letter is used by some job seekers in place of a resume and cover letter. (See Exhibit 2.5.) The purpose of this type of document is to

---

Exhibit 2.5

Broadcast Letter

TRICIA A. SWAIN
27 Parker Street
Rumney, IL 60615
(812) 555-1844

Mr. Niles Lee Perkins, Administrator   June 6, 1998
Webster Nursing Homes, Inc.
Box 270, Rt. 109
Danvers, MA 29401

Dear Mr. Perkins,

   I am writing to you because your organization may be in need of an administrator with my experience, education, and training. My long-term goal is to work in a management role in the area of patient admissions, discharge, and transfer services, developing and delivering quality of care with a strong "bottom line" orientation. Today's health-care marketplace challenges us to continue to provide the highest level of patient services within the confines of increasingly restrictive third-party payments. I feel

continued

continued

well prepared to contribute to your excellent management team as they work hard to keep Webster Nursing Homes ahead of tomorrow's health-care challenges. Some highlights of my experience that might particularly interest you include:

- A serious interest in health care. I have volunteered more than 400 hours in the medical records department of my local hospital and served as college representative to the board of directors.

- My internship with a major hospital in the state focused on queuing problems and delays in operating room scheduling. My recommendations were adopted.

- As a peer counselor here on campus, I have developed excellent listening and counseling skills, qualities I feel are crucial to today's health-care administrator.

- I have excellent research, analytical, and computer software skills, including database and spreadsheet experience. My writing has been consistently recognized throughout college for its clarity and style.

I received my bachelor of science degree in political science from White Mountain College in May of 1998.

It would be a pleasure to review my qualifications with you in a personal interview at some mutually convenient time. I will call your office at the end of next week to make arrangements. I look forward to discussing career opportunities with Webster Nursing Homes, Inc.

Sincerely,

Tricia A. Swain

make a number of potential employers aware of the availability and expertise of the job seeker. Because the broadcast letter is mass-mailed (500 to 600 employers), the amount of work required may not be worth the return for many people. If you choose to mail out a broadcast letter, you can expect to receive a response from 2 to 5 percent, at best, of the organizations that receive your letter.

This type of document is most often used by individuals who have an extensive and quantifiable work history. College students often do not have the credentials and work experience to support using a broadcast letter, and most will find it difficult to effectively quantify a slim work history.

A broadcast letter is generally four paragraphs (one page) long. The first paragraph should immediately gain the attention of the reader and state some unusual accomplishment or skill that would be of benefit to the organization. It also states the reason for the letter. Details of the sender's work history are revealed in the third paragraph. These can appear in paragraph form or as a bulleted list. Education and other qualifications or credentials are then described. Finally, the job seeker indicates what he or she will do to follow up on the letter, which usually is a follow-up call one to two weeks after the letter is sent.

RESUME PRODUCTION AND OTHER TIPS

If you have the option and convenience of using a laser printer, you may want to initially produce a limited number of copies in case you want or need to make changes on your resume.

Resume paper color should be carefully chosen. You should consider the types of employers who will receive your resume and the types of positions for which you are applying. Use white or ivory paper for traditional or conservative employers or for higher-level positions.

Black ink on sharply white paper can be harsh on the reader's eyes. Think about an ivory or cream paper that will provide less contrast and be easier to read. Pink, green, and blue tints should generally be avoided.

Many resume writers buy packages of matching envelopes and cover sheet stationery that, although not absolutely necessary, does convey a professional impression.

If you'll be producing many cover letters at home, be sure you have high-quality printing equipment, whether it be computerized or standard typewriter equipment. Learn standard envelope formats for business and retain a copy of every cover letter you send out. You can use it to take notes of any telephone conversations that may occur.

If attending a job fair, women generally can fold their resume in thirds lengthwise and find it fits into a clutch bag or envelope-style purse. Both men and women will have no trouble if they carry a briefcase. For men without a briefcase, carry the resume in a nicely covered legal-size pad holder or fold it in half lengthwise and place it inside your suitcoat pocket, taking care it doesn't "float" outside your collar.

THE COVER LETTER

The cover letter provides you with the opportunity to tailor your resume by telling the prospective employer how you can be a benefit to the organization. It will allow you to highlight aspects of your background that are not already discussed in your resume and that might be especially relevant to the organization you are contacting or to the position you are seeking. Every resume should have a cover letter enclosed when you send it out. Unlike the resume, which may be mass-produced, a cover letter is most effective when it is individually typed and focused on the particular requirements of the organization in question.

A good cover letter should supplement the resume and motivate the reader to review the resume. The format shown in Exhibit 2.6 is only a suggestion to help you decide what information to include in writing a cover letter.

Exhibit 2.6

Cover Letter Format

Your Street Address
Your Town, State, Zip
Phone Number
Date
Name
Title
Organization
Address

Dear _____:

First Paragraph. In this paragraph state the reason for the letter, name the specific position or type of work you are applying for, and indicate from which resource (career development office, newspaper, contact, employment service) you learned of the opening. The first paragraph can also be used to inquire about future openings.

Second Paragraph. Indicate why you are interested in the position, the company, its products or services, and what you can do for the employer. If you are a recent graduate, explain how

continued

---

continued

your academic background makes you a qualified candidate. Try not to repeat the same information found in the resume.

Third Paragraph. Refer the reader to the enclosed resume for more detailed information.

Fourth Paragraph. In this paragraph say what you will do to follow up on your letter. For example, state that you will call by a certain date to set up an interview or to find out if the company will be recruiting in your area. Finish by indicating your willingness to answer any questions they may have. Be sure you have provided your phone number.

Sincerely,

Type your name

Enclosure

Begin the cover letter with your street address 12 lines down from the top. Leave three to five lines between the date and the name of the person to whom you are addressing the cover letter. Make sure you leave one blank line between the salutation and the body of the letter and between paragraphs. After typing "Sincerely," leave four blank lines and type your name. This should leave plenty of room for your signature. A sample cover letter is shown in Exhibit 2.7.

The following guidelines will help you write good cover letters:

1. Be sure to type your letter; ensure there are no misspellings.

2. Avoid unusual typefaces, such as script.

3. Address the letter to an individual, using the person's name and title. To obtain this information, call the company. If answering a blind newspaper advertisement, address the letter "To Whom It May Concern" or omit the salutation.

4. Be sure your cover letter directly indicates the position you are applying for and tells why you are qualified to fill it.

5. Send the original letter, not a photocopy, with your resume. Keep a copy for your records.

Exhibit 2.7

Sample Cover Letter

13 Locust Street
San Diego, CA 98021
(312) 555-1111
October 12, 1998

Mr. Ken Kochien
Director of Development
Nature Conservancy Preserves
22 Main Street
Lockport, CA 98772

Dear Mr. Kochien:

In May of 1999 I will graduate from the San Diego campus of University College with a bachelor's degree in political science. I read of your opening for a capital campaign manager in *Community Jobs*, and I am very interested in the possibilities it offers. I am writing to explore the opportunity for employment with the Nature Conservancy Preserves.

The advertisement indicated that you were looking for someone capable of coordinating meetings, producing campaign materials and donor acknowledgments. I believe my resume outlines a work and education history that you will find interesting and relevant. Beginning with office duties and logistics for a renowned science conference for two summers early in high school, I gained some advertising and graphics experience with a local newspaper and my writing skills were polished working on our college weekly newspaper. Courses in psychology have added to my major course work, and I had some excellent relevant experience working in our campus admissions office. I am productive, focused, and capable of producing high-quality work under time constraints.

As you will see by the enclosed resume, I have had exposure to considerable technology here at college and am thoroughly familiar with all the software and database systems you mention in your ad. In addition, I have good spreadsheet experience and my word processing skills are excellent.

continued

continued

I would like to meet with you to discuss how my education and experience would be consistent with your needs. I will contact your office next week to discuss the possibility of an interview. In the meantime, if you have any questions or require additional information, please contact me at my home, (312) 555-9201.

Sincerely,

Mary Campbell
Enclosure

6. Make your cover letter no more than one page.

7. Include a phone number where you can be reached.

8. Avoid trite language and have someone read it over to react to its tone, content, and mechanics.

9. For your own information, record the date you send out each letter and resume.

CHAPTER THREE

RESEARCHING CAREERS

· ·

Many political science majors make their degree choice with the expectation that their degree will be the ticket to a job after graduation. But "political science" is a vast field, populated with hundreds of job titles you have never heard before. You know that a political science major has given you an overview of governmental systems, political philosophy, and related subjects. However, you still may be confused as to exactly what kinds of jobs you can do with your degree and what kinds of organizations will hire you. Are Congressional staff jobs reserved only for political science majors? Where does a political science major fit into a state government agency, planning agency, or nonprofit organization?

· ·

WHAT DO THEY CALL THE JOB YOU WANT?

There is every reason to be unaware. One reason for confusion is perhaps a mistaken assumption that a college education provides job training. In most cases it does not. Of course, applied fields such as engineering, management, or education provide specific skills for the workplace, whereas most liberal arts degrees simply provide an education. A liberal arts education exposes you to numerous fields of study and teaches you quantitative reasoning, critical thinking, writing, and speaking, all of which can be successfully applied to a number of different job fields. But it still remains up to you to choose a job field and to learn how to articulate the benefits of your education in a way the employer will appreciate.

As indicated in Chapter 1 on self-assessment, your first task is to understand and value what parts of that education you enjoyed and were good at and would continue to enjoy in your life's work. Did your writing courses encourage you in your ability to express yourself in writing? Did you enjoy the research process, and did you find your work was well received? Did you enjoy any of your required quantitative subjects like algebra or calculus?

The answers to questions such as these provide clues to skills and interests you bring to the employment market over and above the credential of your degree. In fact, it is not an overstatement to suggest that most employers who demand a college degree immediately look beyond that degree to you as a person and your own individual expression of what you like to do and think you can do for them, regardless of your major.

COLLECTING JOB TITLES

The world of employment is a big place, and even seasoned veterans of the job hunt can be surprised about what jobs are to be found in what organizations. You need to become a bit of an explorer and adventurer and be willing to try a variety of techniques to begin a list of possible occupations that might use your talents and education. Once you have a list of possibilities that you are interested in and qualified for, you can move on to find out what kinds of organizations have these job titles.

Not every employer seeking to hire someone with a political science degree may be equally desirable to you. Some employment environments may be more attractive to you than others. A political science major considering government service could do that as a civil servant, member of the armed services, elected representative, or diplomat. Though jobs might involve similar skills, each environment presents a different "culture" with associated norms in the pace of work, the interaction with others, and the background and training of those you'll work with or encounter on the job. Even in roles where job titles are quite similar, not all situations will present the same "fit" for you.

If you majored in political science and enjoyed the in-class presentations you did as part of your degree and have developed some strong communication skills, you might naturally think of public affairs within a governmental agency. But political science majors with these same skills and interests go on to work as human resource officers, agency managers, attorneys (after completing law school), legislators, and executives in nonprofit organizations. Each job title in this list can be found in a variety of settings.

•••

Take training, for example. Trainers write policy and procedural manuals and actively teach to assist all levels of employees in mastering various tasks and work-related systems. Trainers exist in all large corporations, banks, consumer goods manufacturers, medical diagnostic equipment firms, sales organizations, and any organization that has processes or materials that need to be presented to and learned by the staff.

In reading job descriptions or want ads for any of these positions, you would find your four-year degree a "must." However, the academic major might be less important than your own individual skills in critical thinking, analysis, report writing, public presentations, and interpersonal communication. Even more important than thinking or knowing you have certain skills is your ability to express those skills concretely and the examples you use to illustrate them to an employer.

The best beginning to a job search is to create a list of job titles you might want to pursue, learn more about the nature of the jobs behind those titles, and then discover what kinds of employers hire for those positions. In the following section we'll teach you how to build a job title directory to use in your job search.

Developing a Job Title Directory That Works for You

A job title directory is simply a complete list of all the job titles you are interested in, are intrigued by, or think you are qualified for. Combining the understanding gained through self-assessment with your own individual interests and the skills and talents you've acquired with your degree, you'll soon start to read and recognize a number of occupational titles that seem right for you. There are several resources you can use to develop your list, including computer searches, books, and want ads.

Computerized Interest Inventories. One way to begin your search is to identify a number of jobs that call for your degree and the particular skills and interests you identified as part of the self-assessment process. There are excellent interactive computer career guidance programs on the market to help you produce such selected lists of possible job titles. Most of these are available at high schools and colleges and at some larger town and city libraries. Two of the industry leaders are SIGI and DISCOVER. Both allow you to enter interests, values, educational background, and other information to produce lists of possible occupations and industries. Each of the resources listed here will produce different job title lists. Some job titles will appear again and again, while others will be unique to a particular source. Investigate them all!

Reference Books. Books on the market that may be available through your local library, bookstore, or career counseling office also suggest various occupations related to a number of majors. The following are only two of the many good books on the market: *What Can I Do with a Major In . . . ? How to Choose and Use Your College Major,* by Lawrence R. Malnig with Anita Malnig, and *The Occupational Thesaurus. What Can I Do with a Major In . . . ?* lists job titles by academic major and identifies those jobs by their *Dictionary of Occupational Titles (DOT)* code. (See following discussion.)

. . . .

Political science majors can find a variety of job titles in reference works listing occupational titles. In the *Dictionary of Occupational Titles*, for example, a look at major job categories can reveal other jobs. Under the heading for "Occupations in Law and Jurisprudence," the bulk of the information covers different types of lawyers such as district attorneys, patent lawyers, insurance attorneys, probate lawyers, tax attorneys, title attorneys, and other types of lawyers.

At the same time you can also find some positions you may not have thought about. Their work is related to that of lawyers, but duties differ. Position titles include hearing officer, appeals board referee, adjudicator, patent agent,

> appeals referee, contract clerk, legal investigator, and title
> examiner. If legal careers are of interest to you, this source
> adds some depth by suggesting a number of different
> occupational directions.

....

Each job title deserves your consideration. Like the layers of an onion, the search for job titles can go on and on! As you spend time doing this activity, you are actually learning more about the value of your degree. What's important in your search at this point is not to become critical or selective, but rather to develop as long a list of possibilities as you can. Every source used will help you add new and potentially exciting jobs to your growing list.

Want Ads. It has been well publicized that newspaper want ads represent only about 10 to 15 percent of the current job market. Nevertheless, the Sunday want ads can be a great help to you in your search. Although they may not be the best place to look for a job, they can teach the job seeker much about the job market and provide a good education in job descriptions, duties and responsibilities, active industries, and some indication of the volume of job traffic. For our purposes they are a good source for job titles to add to your list.

Read the Sunday want ads in a major market newspaper for several Sundays in a row. Circle and then cut out any and all ads that interest you and seem to call for something close to your education and experience. Remember, because want ads are written for what an organization *hopes* to find, you don't have to meet absolutely every criterion. However, if certain requirements are stated as absolute minimums and you cannot meet them, it's best not to waste your time.

A recent examination of *The Boston Sunday Globe* reveals the following possible occupations for a liberal arts major with some computer skills and limited prior work experience. (This is only a partial list of what was available.)

❑ Admissions representative	❑ Eechnical writer
❑ Salesperson	❑ Eersonnel trainee
❑ Compliance director	❑ GED examiner
❑ Assistant principal gifts writer	❑ Direct mail researcher
❑ Public relations officer	❑ Associate publicist

After performing this exercise for a few Sundays, you'll find you have collected a new library of job titles.

The Sunday want ad exercise is important because these jobs are out in the marketplace. They truly exist, and people with your qualifications are being sought to apply. What's more, many of these advertisements describe the duties and responsibilities of the job advertised and give you a beginning sense of the challenges and opportunities such a position presents. Some will indicate salary, and that will be helpful as well. This information will better define the jobs for you and provide some good material for possible interviews in that field.

Exploring Job Descriptions

Once you've arrived at a solid list of possible job titles that interest you and for which you believe you are somewhat qualified, it's a good idea to do some research on each of these jobs. The preeminent source for such job information is the *Dictionary of Occupational Titles,* or *DOT.* This directory lists every conceivable job and provides excellent up-to-date information on duties and responsibilities, interactions with associates, and day-to-day assignments and tasks. These descriptions provide a thorough job analysis, but they do not consider the possible employers or the environments in which this job may be performed. So, although a position as public relations officer may be well defined in terms of duties and responsibilities, it does not explain the differences in doing public relations work in a college or a hospital or a factory or a bank. You will need to look somewhere else for work settings.

Learning More About Possible Work Settings

After reading some job descriptions, you may choose to edit and revise your list of job titles once again, discarding those you feel are not suitable and keeping those that continue to hold your interest. Or you may wish to keep your list intact and see where these jobs may be located. For example, if you are interested in public relations and you appear to have those skills and the requisite education, you'll want to know what organizations do public relations. How can you find that out? How much income does someone in public relations make a year and what is the employment potential for the field of public relations?

To answer these and many other good questions about your list of job titles, we recommend you try any of the following resources: *Careers Encyclopedia, Career Information Center, College to Career: The Guide to Job Opportunities,* and the *Occupational Outlook Handbook.* Each of these books, in a different way, will help to put the job titles you have selected into an employer context. *VGM's Handbook of Business and Management Careers* contains detailed career descriptions for more than fifty fields. Entries include complete information on duties and responsibilities for individual careers and detailed entry-level requirements. There is information on working conditions and promotional opportunities as well. Salary ranges and career outlook projections are also provided. Perhaps the most extensive discussion is found in the *Occupational Outlook Handbook,* which gives a thorough presentation of the nature of the work, the working conditions, employment statistics, training, other qualifications, and advancement possibilities as well as job outlook and earnings. Related occupations are also detailed, and a select bibliography is provided to help you find additional information.

Continuing with our public relations example, your search through these reference materials would teach you that the public relations jobs you find attractive are available in larger hospitals, financial institutions, most corporations (both consumer goods and industrial goods), media organizations, and colleges and universities.

Networking to Get the Complete Story

You now have not only a list of job titles but also, for each of these job titles, a description of the work involved and a general list of possible employment settings in which to work. You'll want to do some reading and keep talking to friends, colleagues, teachers, and others about the possibilities. Don't neglect to ask if the career office at your college maintains some kind of alumni network. Often such alumni networks will connect you with another graduate from the college who is working in the job title or industry you are seeking information about. These career networkers offer what assistance they can. For some it is a full day "shadowing" the alumnus as he or she goes about the job. Others offer partial day visits, tours, informational interviews, resume reviews, job postings, or, if distance prevents a visit, telephone interviews. As fellow graduates, they'll be frank and informative about their own jobs and prospects in their field.

Take them up on their offer and continue to learn all you can about your own personal list of job titles, descriptions, and employment settings. You'll probably continue to edit and refine this list as you learn more about the realities of the job, the possible salary, advancement opportunities, and supply and demand statistics.

In the next section we'll describe how to find the specific organizations that represent these industries and employers so that you can begin to make contact.

WHERE ARE THESE JOBS, ANYWAY?

Having a list of job titles that you've designed around your own career interests and skills is an excellent beginning. It means you've really thought about who you are and what you are presenting to the employment market. It has caused you to think seriously about the most appealing environments to work in, and you have identified some employer types that represent these environments.

The research and the thinking that you've done this far will be used again and again. It will be helpful in writing your resume and cover letters, in talking about yourself on the telephone to prospective employers, and in answering interview questions.

Now is a good time to begin to narrow the field of job titles and employment sites down to some specific employers to initiate the employment contact.

Finding Out Which Employers Hire People Like You

This section will provide tips, techniques, and specific resources for developing an actual list of specific employers that can be used to make contacts. It is only an outline that you must be prepared to tailor to your own particular needs and according to what you bring to the job search. Once again, it is important to stress the need to communicate with others along the way exactly what you're looking for and what your goals are for the research you're doing. Librarians, employers, career counselors, friends, friends of friends, business contacts, and bookstore staff will all have helpful information on geographically specific and new resources to aid you in locating employers who'll hire you.

Identifying Information Resources

Your interview wardrobe and your new resume may have put a dent in your wallet, but the resources you'll need to pursue your job search are available for free (although you might choose to copy materials on a machine instead of taking notes by hand). The categories of information detailed here are not hard to find and are yours for the browsing.

Numerous resources described in this section will help you identify actual employers. Use all of them or any others that you identify as available in your geographic area. As you become experienced in this process, you'll quickly figure out which information sources are helpful and which are not. If you live in a rural area, a well-planned day trip to a major city that includes a college career office, a large college or city library, state and federal employment centers, a chamber of commerce office, and a well-stocked bookstore can produce valuable results.

There are many excellent resources available to help you identify actual job sites. They are categorized into employer directories (usually indexed by product lines and geographic location), geographically based directories (designed to highlight particular cities, regions, or states), career-specific directories (e.g., *Sports Market Place,* which lists tens of thousands of firms involved with sports), periodicals and newspapers, targeted job posting publications, and videos. This is by no means meant to be a complete list of resources, but rather a starting point for identifying useful resources.

Working from the more general references to highly specific resources, we will provide a basic list to help you begin your search. Many of these you'll find easily available. In some cases reference librarians and others will suggest even better materials for your particular situation. Start to create your own customized bibliography of job search references. Use copying services to save time and to allow you to carry away information about organization mission, location, company officers, phone numbers, and addresses.

Employer Directories. There are many employer directories available to give you the kind of information you need for your job search. Some of our favorites are listed here, but be sure to ask the professionals you are working with to make additional suggestions.

- *America's Corporate Families* identifies many major U.S. ultimate parent companies and displays corporate family linkage of subsidiaries and divisions. Businesses can be identified by their industrial code.

- *Million Dollar Directory: America's Leading Public and Private Companies* lists about 160,000 companies.

- *Moody's* various manuals are intended as guides for investors, so they contain a history of each company. Each manual contains a classification of companies by industries and products.

- *Standard and Poor's Register of Corporations* contains listings for 45,000 businesses, some of which are not listed in the *Million Dollar Directory.*

- *Job Seekers Guide to Private and Public Companies* profiles 15,000 employers in four volumes, each covering a different geographic region. Company entries include contact information, business descriptions, and application procedures.

- *The Career Guide: Dun's Employment Opportunities Directory* lists more than 5,000 large organizations, including hospitals and local governments. Profiles include an overview and history of the employer as well as opportunities, benefits, and contact names. It contains geographic and industrial indexes and indexes by discipline or internship availability. This guide also includes a state-by-state list of professional personnel consultants and their specialties.

❑ *Professional's Job Finder/Government Job Finder/Non-Profits Job Finder* are specific directories of job services, salary surveys, and periodical listings in which advertisements for jobs in the professional, government, or not-for-profit sector are found.

❑ *Opportunities in Nonprofit Organizations* is a VGM career series edition that opens up the world of not-for-profit by helping you match your interest profile to the aims and objectives of scores of nonprofit employers in business, education, health and medicine, social welfare, science and technology, and many others. There is also a special section on fund-raising and development career paths.

❑ *The 100 Best Companies to Sell For* lists companies by industry and provides contact information and describes benefits and corporate culture.

❑ *The 100 Best Companies to Work For in America* rates organizations on several factors including opportunities, job security, and pay.

❑ *Companies That Care* lists organizations that the authors believe are family-friendly. One index organizes information by state.

❑ *Infotrac CD-ROM Business Index* covers business journals and magazines as well as news magazines and can provide information on public and private companies.

❑ *ABI/Inform On Disc* (CD-ROM) indexes articles in more than 800 journals.

Geographically Based Directories. The Job Bank series published by Bob Adams, Inc. contains detailed entries on each area's major employers, including business activity, address, phone number, and hiring contact name. Many listings specify educational backgrounds being sought in potential employees. Each volume contains a solid discussion of each city's or state's major employment sectors. Organizations are also indexed by industry. Job Bank volumes are available for the following places: Atlanta, Boston, Chicago, Denver, Dallas–Ft. Worth, Florida, Houston, Ohio, St. Louis, San Francisco, Seattle, Los Angeles, New York, Detroit, Philadelphia, Minneapolis, the Northwest, and Washington, D.C.

National Job Bank lists employers in every state, along with contact names and commonly hired job categories. Included are many small companies often overlooked by other directories. Companies are also indexed by industry. This publication provides information on educational backgrounds sought and lists company benefits.

Career-Specific Directories. VGM publishes a number of excellent series detailing careers for college graduates. In the *Professional Career Series* are guides to careers in the following fields, among others:

❑ Advertising

❑ Communications

❑ Business

❑ Computers

❑ Health Care

❑ High Tech

Each provides an excellent discussion of the industry, educational requirements for jobs, salary ranges, duties, and projected outlooks for the field.

Another VGM series, *Opportunities In . . .*, has an equally wide range of titles relating to specific majors, such as the following:

❑ *Opportunities in Banking*

❑ *Opportunities in Insurance*

❑ *Opportunities in Federal Government*

❑ *Opportunities in Government Service*

❑ *Opportunities in Journalism*

❑ *Opportunities in Law*

❑ *Opportunities in State and Local Government*

❑ *Opportunities in Teaching*

❑ *Opportunities in Nonprofit Organizations*

Periodicals and Newspapers. Several sources are available to help you locate which journals or magazines carry job advertisements in your field. Other resources help you identify opportunities in other parts of the country.

❑ *Where the Jobs Are: A Comprehensive Directory of 1,200 Journals Listing Career Opportunities* links specific occupational titles to corresponding periodicals that carry job listings for your field.

❑ *Social & Behavioral Sciences Jobs Handbook* contains a periodicals matrix organized by academic discipline and highlights periodicals containing job listings.

- *National Business Employment Weekly* compiles want ads from four regional editions of the *Wall Street Journal.* Most are business and management positions.

- *National Ad Search* reprints ads from seventy-five metropolitan newspapers across the country. Although the focus is on management positions, technical and professional postings are also included. *Caution:* Watch deadline dates carefully on listings because deadlines may have already passed by the time the ad is printed.

- *The Federal Jobs Digest* and *Federal Career Opportunities* list government positions.

- *World Chamber of Commerce Directory* lists addresses for chambers worldwide, state boards of tourism, convention and visitors' bureaus, and economic development organizations.

This list is certainly not exhaustive; use it to begin your job search work.

Targeted Job Posting Publications. Although the resources that follow are national in scope, they are either targeted to one medium of contact (telephone), focused on specific types of jobs, or are less comprehensive than the sources previously listed.

- *Job Hotlines USA* pinpoints more than one thousand hard-to-find telephone numbers for companies and government agencies that use prerecorded job messages and listings. Very few of the telephone numbers listed are toll-free, and sometimes recordings are long, so callers beware!

- *The Job Hunter* is a national biweekly newspaper listing business, arts, media, government, human services, health, community-related, and student services job openings.

- *Current Jobs for Graduates* is a national employment listing for liberal arts professions, including editorial positions, management opportunities, museum work, teaching, and nonprofit work.

- *Environmental Opportunities* serves environmental job interests nationwide by listing administrative, marketing, and human resources positions along with education-related jobs and positions directly related to a degree in an environmental field.

- *Y National Vacancy List* shows YMCA professional vacancies, including development, administration, programming, membership, and recreation postings.

- *ARTSearch is* a national employment service bulletin for the arts, including administration, managerial, marketing, and financial management jobs.

- *Community Jobs* is an employment newspaper for the nonprofit sector that provides a variety of listings, including project manager, canvas director, government relations specialist, community organizer, and program instructor.

- *College Placement Council Annual: A Guide to Employment Opportunities for College Graduates* is an annual guide containing solid job-hunting information and, more importantly, displaying ads from large corporations actively seeking recent college graduates in all majors. Company profiles provide brief descriptions and available employment opportunities. Contact names and addresses are given. Profiles are indexed by organization name, geographic location, and occupation.

Videos. You may be one of the many job seekers who like to get information via a medium other than paper. Many career libraries, public libraries, and career centers in libraries carry an assortment of videos that will help you learn new techniques and get information helpful in the job search. A small sampling of the multitude of videos now available includes the following:

- *The Skills Search* (20 min.) discusses three types of skills important in the workplace, how to present the skills in an interview, and how to respond to problem questions.

- *Effective Answers to Interview Questions* (35 min.) presents two real-life job seekers and shows how they realized the true meaning of interview questions and formulated positive answers.

- *Employer's Expectations* (33 min.) covers three areas that are important to all employers: appearance, dependability, and skills.

- *The Tough New Labor Market of the 1990s* (30 min.) presents labor market facts as well as suggestions on what job seekers should do to gain employment in this market.

- *Dialing for Jobs: Using the Phone in the Job Search* (30 min.) describes how to use the phone effectively to gain information and arrange interviews by following two new graduates as they learn and apply techniques.

Locating Information Resources

An essay by John Case that appeared in the *Boston Globe* (August 25, 1993) alerts both new and seasoned job seekers that the job market is changing, and the old guarantees of lifelong employment no longer hold true. Some of our major corporations, which were once seen as the most prestigious of employment destinations, are now laying off thousands of employees. Middle management is especially hard hit in downsizing situations. On the other side of the coin, smaller, more entrepreneurial firms are adding employees and realizing enormous profit margins. The geography of the new job market is unfamiliar, and the terrain is much harder to map. New and smaller firms can mean different kinds of jobs and new job titles. The successful job seeker will keep an open mind about where he or she might find employment and what that employment might be called.

In order to become familiar with this new terrain, you will need to undertake some research, which can be done at any of the following locations:

- Public libraries

- Business organizations

- Employment agencies

- Bookstores

- Career libraries

Each one of these places offers a collection of resources that will help you get the information you need.

As you meet and talk with service professionals at all these sites, be sure to let them know what you're doing. Inform them of your job search, what you've already accomplished, and what you're looking for. The more people who know you're job seeking, the greater the possibility that someone will have information or know someone who can help you along your way.

Public Libraries. Large city libraries, college and university libraries, and even well-supported town library collections contain a variety of resources to help you conduct a job search. It is not uncommon for libraries to have separate "vocational choices" sections with books, tapes, and associated materials relating to job search and selection. Some are now even making resume creation software available for use by patrons.

Some of the publications we name throughout this book are expensive reference items that are rarely purchased by individuals. In addition, libraries carry a wide range of newspapers and telephone yellow pages as well as the usual array of books. If resources are not immediately available, many libraries have loan arrangements with other facilities and can make information available to you relatively quickly.

Take advantage of not only the reference collections, but also the skilled and informed staff. Let them know exactly what you are looking for, and they'll have their own suggestions. You'll be visiting the library frequently, and the reference staff will soon come to know who you are and what you're working on. They'll be part of your job search network!

Business Organizations. Chambers of Commerce, Offices of New Business Development, Councils on Business and Industry, Small Business Administration (SBA) offices, and professional associations can all provide geographically specific lists of companies and organizations that have hiring needs. They also have an array of other available materials, including visitors' guides and regional fact books that provide additional employment information.

These agencies serve to promote local and regional businesses and ensure their survival and success. Although these business organizations do not advertise job openings or seek employees for their members, they may be very aware of staffing needs among their member firms. In your visits to each of these locations, spend some time with the personnel getting to know who they are and what they do. Let them know of your job search and your intentions regarding employment. You may be surprised and delighted at the information they may provide.

Employment Agencies. Employment agencies (including state and federal employment offices), professional "headhunters" or executive search firms, and some private career counselors can provide direct leads to job openings. Don't overlook these resources. If you are mounting a complete job search program and want to ensure that you are covering the potential market for employers, consider the employment agencies in your territory. Some of these organizations work contractually with several specific firms and may have access that is unavailable to you. Others may be particularly well-informed about supply and demand in particular industries or geographic locations.

In the case of professional (commercial) employment agencies, which include those executive recruitment firms labeled "headhunters," you should be cautious about entering into any binding contractual agreement. Before doing so, be sure to get the information you need to decide whether their services can be of use to you. Questions to ask include the following: Who pays the fee when employment is obtained? Are there any other fees or costs associated with this service? What is their placement rate? Can you see a list of previous clients and can you talk to any for references? Do they typically work with entry-level job seekers? Do they tend to focus on particular kinds of employment or industries?

A few cautions are in order, however, when you work with professional agencies. Remember, the professional employment agency is, in most cases, paid by the hiring organization. Naturally, their interest and attention is largely directed to the employer, not to the candidate. Of course, they want to provide good candidates to guarantee future contracts, but they are less interested in the job seeker than the employer.

For teacher candidates there are a number of good placement firms that charge the prospective teacher, not the employer. This situation has evolved over time as a result of supply and demand and financial structuring of most school systems, which cannot spend money on recruiting teachers. Usually these firms charge a nonrefundable administrative fee and, upon successful placement, require a fee based on percentage of salary, which may range from 10 to 20 percent of annual compensation. Often, this can be repaid over a number of months. Check your contract carefully.

State and federal employment offices are no-fee services that maintain extensive "job boards" and can provide detailed specifications for each job advertised and help with application forms. Because government employment application forms are detailed, keep a master copy along with copies of all additional documentation (resumes, educational transcripts, military discharge papers, proof of citizenship, etc.). Successive applications may require separate filings. Visit these offices as frequently as you can because most deal with applicants on a "walk-in" basis and will not telephone prospective candidates or maintain files of job seekers. Check your telephone book for the address of the nearest state and federal offices.

One type of employment service that causes much confusion among job seekers is the outplacement firm. Their advertisements tend to suggest they will put you in touch with the "hidden job market." They use advertising phrases such as "We'll work with you until you get that job" or "Maximize your earnings and career opportunities." In fact, if you read the fine print on these ads, you will notice these firms must state they are "Not an employment agency." These firms are, in fact, corporate and private outplacement counseling agencies whose work involves resume editing, counseling to provide leads for jobs, interview skills training, and all the other aspects of hiring preparation. They do this for a fee, sometimes in the thousands of dollars range, which is paid by you, the client. Some of these firms have good reputations and provide excellent materials and techniques. Most, however, provide a service you as a college student or graduate can receive free from your alma mater or through a reciprocity agreement between your college and a college or university located closer to your current address.

Bookstores. Any well-stocked bookstore will carry some job search books that are worth buying. Some major stores will even have an extensive section devoted to materials, including excellent videos, related to the job search process. Several possibilities are listed in the following sections. You will also find copies of local newspapers and business magazines. The one advantage that is provided by resources purchased at a bookstore is that you can read and work with the information in the comfort of your own home and do not have to conform to the hours of operation of a library, which can present real difficulties if you are working full time as you seek employment. A few minutes spent browsing in a bookstore might be a beneficial break from your job search activities and turn up valuable resources.

Career Libraries. Career libraries, which are found in career centers at colleges and universities and sometimes within large public libraries, contain a unique blend of the job search resources housed in other settings. In addition, career libraries often purchase a number of job listing publications, each of which targets a specific industry or type of job. You may find job listings specifically for entry-level positions for political science majors. Ask about job posting newsletters or newspapers specifically focused on careers in the area that most interests you. Each center will be unique, but you are certain to discover some good sources of jobs.

Most college career libraries now hold growing collections of video material on specific industries and on aspects of your job search process, including dress and appearance, how to manage the luncheon or dinner interview, how to be effective at a job fair, and many other specific titles. Some larger corporations produce handsome video materials detailing the variety of career paths and opportunities available in their organizations.

Some career libraries also house computer-based career planning and information systems. These interactive computer programs help you to clarify your values and interests and will combine that with your education to provide possible job titles and industry locations. Some even contain extensive lists of graduate school programs.

One specific kind of service a career library will be able to direct you to is computerized job search services. These services, of which there are many, are run by private companies, individual colleges, or consortiums of colleges. They attempt to match qualified job candidates with potential employers. The candidate submits a resume (or an application) to the service. This information (which can be categorized into hundreds of separate "fields" of data) is entered into a computer database. Your information is then compared with the information from employers about what they desire in a prospective employee. If there is a "match" between what they want and what you have indicated you can offer, the job search service or the employer will contact you directly to continue the process.

Computerized job search services can complement an otherwise complete job search program. They are *not*, however, a substitute for the kinds of activities described in this book. They are essentially passive operations that are random in nature. If you have not listed skills, abilities, traits, experiences, or education *exactly* as an employer has listed its needs, there is simply no match.

Consult with the staff members at the career libraries you use. These professionals have been specifically trained to meet the unique needs you present. Often you can just drop in and receive help with general questions, or you may want to set up an appointment to speak one-on-one with a career counselor to gain special assistance.

Every career library is different in size and content, but each can provide valuable information for the job search. Some may even provide some limited counseling. If you have not visited the career library at your college or alma mater, call and ask if these collections are still available for your use. Be sure to ask about other services that you can use as well.

If you are not near your own college as you work on your job search, call the career office and inquire about reciprocal agreements with other colleges that are closer to where you live. Very often your own alma mater can arrange for you to use a limited menu of services at another school. This typically would include access to a career library and job posting information and might include limited counseling.

CHAPTER FOUR

NETWORKING

etworking is the process of deliberately establishing relationships to get career-related information or to alert potential employers that you are available for work. Networking is critically important to today's job seeker for two reasons: it will help you get the information you need, and it can help you find out about *all* of the available jobs.

Getting the Information You Need

Networkers will review your resume and give you candid feedback on its effectiveness. They will talk about the job you are looking for and give you a candid appraisal of how they see your strengths and weaknesses. If they have a good sense of the industry or the employment sector for that job, you'll get their feelings on future trends in the industry as well. Some networkers will be very candid about salaries, job hunting techniques, and suggestions for your job search strategy. Many have been known to place calls right from the interview desk to friends and associates that might be interested in you. Each networker will make his or her own contribution, and each will be valuable.

Because organizations must evolve to adapt to current global market needs, the information provided by decision makers within various organizations will be critical to your success as a new job market entrant. Networking can help you find out about trends currently affecting the industries under your consideration.

Finding Out About All of the Available Jobs

Secondly, not every job that is available at this very moment is advertised for potential applicants to see. This is called the *hidden job market*. Only 15 to

20 percent of all jobs are formally advertised, which means that 80 to 85 percent of available jobs do not appear in published channels. Networking will help you become more knowledgeable about all the employment opportunities available during your job search period.

Although someone you might talk to today doesn't know of any openings within his or her organization, tomorrow or next week or next month an opening may occur. If you've taken the time to show an interest in and knowledge of their organization, if you've shown the company representative how you can help achieve organizational goals and that you can fit into the organization, you'll be one of the first candidates considered for the position.

Networking: A Proactive Approach

Networking is a proactive rather than a reactive approach. You, as a job seeker, are expected to initiate a certain level of activity on your own behalf; you cannot afford to simply respond to jobs listed in the newspaper. Being proactive means building a network of contacts that includes informed and interested decision makers who will provide you with up-to-date knowledge of the current job market and increase your chances of finding out about employment opportunities appropriate for your interests, experience, and level of education.

An old axiom of networking says "You are only two phone calls away from the information you need." In other words, by talking to enough people, you will quickly come across someone who can offer you help. Start with your professors. Each of them probably has a wide circle of contacts. In their work and travel they might have met someone who can help you or direct you to someone who can.

Control and the Networking Process

In deliberately establishing relationships, the process of networking begins with you in control—*you* are contacting specific individuals. As your network expands and you establish a set of professional relationships, your search for information or jobs will begin to move outside of your total control. A part of the networking process involves others assisting you by gathering information for you or recommending you as a possible job candidate. As additional people become a part of your networking system, you will have less knowledge about activities undertaken on your behalf; you will undoubtedly be contacted by individuals whom you did not initially approach. If you want to function effectively in surprise situations, you must be prepared at all times to talk with strangers about the informational or employment needs that motivated you to become involved in the networking process.

PREPARING TO NETWORK

In deliberately establishing relationships, maximize your efforts by organizing your approach. Five specific areas in which you can organize your efforts include reviewing your self-assessment, reviewing your research on job sites and organizations, deciding who it is you want to talk to, keeping track of all your efforts, and creating your self-promotion tools.

Review Your Self-Assessment

Your self-assessment is as important a tool in preparing to network as it has been in other aspects of your job search. You have carefully evaluated your personal traits, personal values, economic needs, longer-term goals, skill base, preferred skills, and underdeveloped skills. During the networking process you will be called upon to communicate what you know about yourself and relate it to the information or job you seek. Be sure to review the exercises that you completed in the self-assessment section of this book in preparation for networking. We've explained that you need to assess what skills you have acquired from your major that are of general value to an employer and to be ready to express those in ways employers can appreciate as useful in their own organizations.

Review Researching Job Sites and Organizations

In addition, individuals assisting you will expect that you'll have at least some background information on the occupation or industry of interest to you. Refer to the appropriate sections of this book and other relevant publications to acquire the background information necessary for effective networking. They'll explain how to identify not only the job titles that might be of interest to you, but also what kinds of organizations employ people to do that job. You will develop some sense of working conditions and expectations about duties and responsibilities—all of which will be of help in your networking interviews.

Decide Who It Is You Want to Talk To

Networking cannot begin until you decide who it is that you want to talk to and, in general, what type of information you hope to gain from your contacts. Once you know this, it's time to begin developing a list of contacts. Five useful sources for locating contacts are described here.

College Alumni Network. Most colleges and universities have created a formal network of alumni and friends of the institution who are particularly interested in helping currently enrolled students and graduates of their alma mater gain employment-related information.

....

> Because the political science major covers such a broad spectrum of human activity, you'll find political science majors employed in every sector of the economy: not only government but also business and nonprofit. The diversity of employment as evidenced by an alumni list from your college or university should be encouraging to the political science graduate. Among such a diversified group, there are likely to be scores you would enjoy talking with. Some might be working quite far from you, but that does not preclude a telephone call, letter, or E-mail message.

....

It is usually a simple process to make use of an alumni network. You need only visit the alumni or career office at your college or university and follow the procedure that has been established. Often, you will simply complete a form indicating your career goals and interests and you will be given the names of appropriate individuals to contact. In many cases staff members will coach you on how to make the best use of the limited time these alumni contacts may have available for you.

Alumni networkers may provide some combination of the following services: day-long shadowing experiences, telephone interviews, in-person interviews, information on relocating to given geographic areas, internship information, suggestions on graduate school study, and job vacancy notices.

....

> What a valuable experience! If you are interested in a nonprofit administrative position, you may be concerned about your degree preparation and whether you would be considered eligible to work in this field. Spending a day with an alumnus who works as an administrator for a nonprofit, asking questions about his or her educational preparation and training, will give you a more concrete view of the possibilities for your degree. Observing

firsthand how this person does the job and exactly what
the job entails is a far better decision criteria for you than
just reading on the subject could possibly provide.

....

Present and Former Supervisors. If you believe you are on good terms with
present or former job supervisors, they may be an excellent resource for providing information or directing you to appropriate resources that would have
information related to your current interests and needs. Additionally, these
supervisors probably belong to professional organizations, which they might
be willing to utilize to get information for you.

....

If, for example, you were interested in working as a legislative assistant for a member of your state legislature,
and you are currently working as a program director at
the local chamber of commerce, talk with your supervisor or the executive director. He or she will probably
know at least one state delegate or senator or will know
influential members of the chamber who have strong
political contacts. At least one of these people will probably be able to provide you with names and business telephone numbers of not only legislators, but current staff
members. You could then begin the networking process.

....

Employers in Your Area. Although you may be interested in working in a geographic location different from the one where you currently reside, don't overlook the value of the knowledge and contacts those around you are able to
provide. Use the local telephone directory and newspaper to identify the types
of organizations you are thinking of working for or professionals who have
the kinds of jobs you are interested in. Recently, a call made to a local hospital's financial administrator for information on working in health care
financial administration yielded more pertinent information on training
seminars, regional professional organizations, and potential employment sites
than a national organization was willing to provide.

Employers in Geographic Areas Where You Hope to Work. If you are thinking about relocating, identifying prospective employers or informational contacts in this new location will be critical to your success. Many resources are available to help you locate contact names. These include the yellow pages directory, the local newspapers, local or state business publications, and local chambers of commerce.

Professional Associations and Organizations. Professional associations and organizations can provide valuable information in several areas: career paths that you may not have considered, qualifications relating to those career choices, publications that list current job openings, and workshops or seminars that will enhance your professional knowledge and skills. They can also be excellent sources for background information on given industries: their health, current problems, and future challenges.

There are several excellent resources available to help you locate professional associations and organizations that would have information to meet your needs. Two especially useful publications are the *Encyclopedia of Associations* and the *National Trade and Professional Associations of the United States.*

Keep Track of All Your Efforts

It can be difficult, almost impossible, to remember all the details related to each contact you make during the networking process, so you will want to develop a record-keeping system that works for you. Formalize this process by using a notebook or index cards to organize the information you gather. Begin by creating a list of the people or organizations you want to contact. Record the contact's name, address, telephone number, and what information you hope to gain. Each entry might look something like this:

Contact Name	Address	Phone #	Purpose
Mr. Tim Keefe	Wrigley Bldg.		
Dir. of Mines	Suite 72	555-8906	Resume screen

Once you have created this initial list, it will be helpful to keep more detailed information as you begin to actually make the contacts. Using the Network Contact Record form in Exhibit 4.1, keep good information on all your network contacts. They'll appreciate your recall of details of your meetings and conversations, and the information will help you to focus your networking efforts.

Exhibit 4.1

Network Contact Record

Name: Be certain your spelling is absolutely correct.

Title: Pick up a business card to be certain of the correct title.

Employing organization: Note any parent company or subsidiaries.

Business mailing address: This is often different from the street address.

Business telephone number: Include area code/alternative numbers/fax/E-mail.

Source for this contact: Who referred you, and what is their relationship?

Date of call or letter: Use plenty of space here to record multiple phone calls or visits, other employees you may have met, names of secretaries/ receptionists, etc.

Content of discussion: Keep enough notes here to remind you of the substance of your visits and telephone conversations in case some time elapses between contacts.

Follow-up necessary to continue working with this contact: Your contact may request that you send him or her some materials or direct you to contact an associate. Note any such instructions or assignments in this space.

Name of additional networker: Here you would record the
Address: names and phone numbers of
Phone: additional contacts met at this
Name of additional networker: employer's site. Often you will
Address: be introduced to many people,
Phone: some of whom may indicate
Name of additional networker: a willingness to help in your
Address: job search.
Phone:

Date thank-you note written: May help to date your next contact.

Follow-up action taken: Phone calls, visits, additional notes.

continued

> continued
>
> **Other miscellaneous notes:** Record any other additional interaction you think may be important to remember in working with this networking client. You will want this form in front of you when telephoning or just before and after a visit.

Create Your Self-Promotion Tools

There are two types of promotional tools that are used in the networking process. The first is a resume and cover letter, and the second is a one-minute "infomercial," which may be given over the telephone or in person.

Techniques for writing an effective resume and cover letter are covered in Chapter 2. Once you have reviewed that material and prepared these important documents, you will have created one of your self-promotion tools.

The one-minute infomercial will demand that you begin tying your interests, abilities, and skills to the people or organizations you want to network with. Think about your goal for making the contact to help you understand what you should say about yourself. You should be able to express yourself easily and convincingly. If, for example, you are contacting an alumnus of your institution to obtain the names of possible employment sites in a distant city, be prepared to discuss why you are interested in moving to that location, the types of jobs you are interested in, and the skills and abilities you possess that will make you a qualified candidate.

To create a meaningful one-minute infomercial, write it out, practice it if it will be a spoken presentation, rewrite it, and practice it again if necessary until expressing yourself comes easily and is convincing.

Here's a simplified example of an infomercial for use over the telephone:

> Hello, Mr. Hamrick? My name is Cindy Lewis. I am a recent graduate of Gulf Shores College, and I wish to enter the nonprofit field. I feel confident I have many of the skills I understand are valued for managers in nonprofit settings. I have a strong quantitative background with good research and computer skills. In addition, I

have excellent interpersonal skills and am known as a compassionate, caring individual. I understand these are valuable traits in your line of work!

Mr. Hamrick, I'm calling you because I still need more information about nonprofit management and where I might fit in. I'm hoping you'll have time to sit down with me for about half an hour and discuss your perspective on careers in nonprofit management with me. There are so many possible employers to approach, and I am seeking some advice on which might be the best bet for my particular combination of skills and experience.

Would you be willing to do that for me? I would greatly appreciate it. I am available most mornings, if that's convenient for you.

Other effective self-promotion tools include portfolios for those in the arts, writing professions, or teaching. Portfolios show examples of work, photographs of projects or classroom activities, or certificates and credentials that are job related. There may not be an opportunity to use the portfolio during an interview, and it is not something that should be left with the organization. It is designed to be explained and displayed by the creator. However, during some networking meetings, there may be an opportunity to illustrate a point or strengthen a qualification by exhibiting the portfolio.

BEGINNING THE NETWORKING PROCESS

Set the Tone for Your Contacts

It can be useful to establish "tone words" for any communications you embark upon. Before making your first telephone call or writing your first letter, decide what you want your contact to think of you. If you are networking to try to obtain a job, your tone words might include words like *genuine, informed,* and *self-knowledgeable.* When trying to acquire information, your tone words may have a slightly different focus, such as *courteous, organized, focused,* and *well-spoken.* Use the tone words you establish for your contacts to guide you through the networking process.

Honestly Express Your Intentions

When contacting individuals, it is important to be honest about your reasons for making the contact. Establish your purpose in your own mind and be able and ready to articulate it concisely. Determine an initial agenda, whether it be informational questioning or self-promotion, present it to your contact, and be ready to respond immediately. If you don't adequately prepare before initiating your contacts, you may find yourself at a disadvantage if you're asked to immediately begin your informational interview or self-promotion during the first phone conversation or visit.

Start Networking Within Your Circle of Confidence

Once you have organized your approach—by utilizing specific researching methods, creating a system for keeping track of the people you will contact, and developing effective self-promotion tools—you are ready to begin networking. The best place to begin networking is by talking with a group of people you trust and feel comfortable with. This group is usually made up of your family, friends, and career counselors. No matter who is in this inner circle, they will have a special interest in seeing you succeed in your job search. In addition, because they will be easy to talk to, you should try taking some risks in terms of practicing your information-seeking approach. Gain confidence in talking about the strengths you bring to an organization and the underdeveloped skills you feel hinder your candidacy. Be sure to review the section on self-assessment for tips on approaching each of these areas. Ask for critical but constructive feedback from the people in your circle of confidence on the letters you write and the one-minute infomercial you have developed. Evaluate whether you want to make the changes they suggest, then practice the changes on others within this circle.

Stretch the Boundaries of Your Networking Circle of Confidence

Once you have refined the promotional tools you will use to accomplish your networking goals, you will want to make additional contacts. Because you will not know most of these people, it will be a less comfortable activity to undertake. The practice that you gained with your inner circle of trusted friends should have prepared you to now move outside of that comfort zone.

It is said that any information a person needs is only two phone calls away, but the information cannot be gained until you (1) make a reasonable guess about who might have the information you need and (2) pick up the telephone to make the call. Using your network list that includes alumni, instructors, supervisors, employers, and associations, you can begin preparing your list of questions that will allow you to get the information you need. Review the question list shown below and then develop a list of your own.

Questions You Might Want to Ask

1. In the position you now hold, what do you do on a typical day?

2. What are the most interesting aspects of your job?

3. What part of your work do you consider dull or repetitious?

4. What were the jobs you had that led to your present position?

5. How long does it usually take to move from one step to the next in this career path?

6. What is the top position to which you can aspire in this career path?

7. What is the next step in *your* career path?

8. Are there positions in this field that are similar to your position?

9. What are the required qualifications and training for entry-level positions in this field?

10. Are there specific courses a student should take to be qualified to work in this field?

11. What are the entry-level jobs in this field?

12. What types of training are provided to persons entering this field?

13. What are the salary ranges your organization typically offers to entry-level candidates for positions in this field?

14. What special advice would you give a person entering this field?

15. Do you see this field as a growing one?

16. How do you see the content of the entry-level jobs in this field changing over the next two years?

17. What can I do to prepare myself for these changes?

18. What is the best way to obtain a position that will start me on a career in this field?

19. Do you have any information on job specifications and descriptions that I may have?

20. What related occupational fields would you suggest I explore?

21. How could I improve my resume for a career in this field?

22. Who else would you suggest I talk to, both in your organization and in other organizations?

Questions You Might Have to Answer

In order to communicate effectively, you must anticipate questions that will be asked of you by the networkers you contact. Review the list below and see if you can easily answer each of these questions. If you cannot, it may be time to revisit the self-assessment process.

1. Where did you get my name, or how did you find out about this organization?

2. What are your career goals?

3. What kind of job are you interested in?

4. What do you know about this organization and this industry?

5. How do you know you're prepared to undertake an entry-level position in this industry?

6. What course work have you taken that is related to your career interests?

7. What are your short-term career goals?

8. What are your long-term career goals?

9. Do you plan to obtain additional formal education?

10. What contributions have you made to previous employers?

11. Which of your previous jobs have you enjoyed the most, and why?

12. What are you particularly good at doing?

13. What shortcomings have you had to face in previous employment?

14. What are your three greatest strengths?

15. Describe how comfortable you feel with your communication style.

General Networking Tips

Make Every Contact Count. Setting the tone for each interaction is critical. Approaches that will help you communicate in an effective way include politeness, being appreciative of time provided to you, and being prepared and thorough. Remember, *everyone* within an organization has a circle of influence, so be prepared to interact effectively with each person you encounter in the networking process, including secretarial and support staff. Many information or job seekers have thwarted their own efforts by being rude to some individuals they encountered as they networked because they made the incorrect assumption that certain persons were unimportant.

Sometimes your contacts may be surprised at their ability to help you. After meeting and talking with you, they might think they have not offered much in the way of help. A day or two later, however, they may make a contact that would be useful to you and refer you to it.

With Each Contact, Widen Your Circle of Networkers. Always leave an informational interview with the names of at least two more people who can help you get the information or job that you are seeking. Don't be shy about asking for additional contacts; networking is all about increasing the number of people you can interact with to achieve your goals.

Make Your Own Decisions. As you talk with different people and get answers to the questions you pose, you may hear conflicting information or get conflicting suggestions. Your job is to listen to these "experts" and decide what information and which suggestions will help you achieve *your* goals. Only implement those suggestions that you believe will work for you.

SHUTTING DOWN YOUR NETWORK

As you achieve the goals that motivated your networking activity—getting the information you need or the job you want—the time will come to inactivate all or parts of your network. As you do so, be sure to tell your primary supporters about your change in status. Call or write to each one of them and give them as many details about your new status as you feel is necessary to maintain a positive relationship.

Because a network takes on a life of its own, activity undertaken on your behalf will continue even after you cease your efforts. As you get calls or are contacted in some fashion, be sure to inform these networkers about your change in status, and thank them for assistance they have provided.

Information on the latest employment trends indicates that workers will change jobs or careers several times in their lifetime. If you carefully and thoughtfully conduct your networking activities now, you will have solid experience when you need to network again.

CHAPTER FIVE

INTERVIEWING

*C*ertainly, there can be no one part of the job search process more fraught with anxiety and worry than the interview. Yet seasoned job seekers welcome the interview and will often say "Just get me an interview and I'm on my way!" They understand that the interview is crucial to the hiring process and equally crucial for them, as job candidates, to have the opportunity of a personal dialogue to add to what the employer may already have learned from a resume, cover letter, and telephone conversations.

Believe it or not, the interview is to be welcomed, and even enjoyed! It is a perfect opportunity for you, the candidate, to sit down with an employer and express yourself and display who you are and what you want. Of course, it takes thought and planning and a little strategy; after all, it *is* a job interview! But it can be a positive, if not pleasant, experience and one you can look back on and feel confident about your performance and effort.

For many new job seekers, a job, any job, seems a wonderful thing. But seasoned interview veterans know that the job interview is an important step for both sides—the employer and the candidate—to see what each has to offer and whether there is going to be a "fit" of personalities, work styles, and attitudes. And it is this concept of balance in the interview, that both sides have important parts to play, that holds the key to success in mastering this aspect of the job search strategy.

Try to think of the interview as a conversation between two interested and equal partners. You both have important, even vital, information to deliver and to learn. Of course, there's no denying the employer has some leverage, especially in the initial interview for recruitment or any interview scheduled by the candidate and not the recruiter. That should not prevent the interviewee from seeking to play an equal part in what should be a fair exchange of information. Too often the untutored candidate allows the interview to become one-sided. The employer asks all the questions and the candidate simply responds. The ideal would be for two mutually interested parties to sit down and discuss possibilities for each. For this is a *conversation of significance,* and it requires pre-interview preparation, thought about the tone of the interview, and planning of the nature and details of the information to be exchanged.

PREPARING FOR THE INTERVIEW

Most initial interviews are about thirty minutes long. Given the brevity, the information that is exchanged ought to be important. The candidate should be delivering material that the employer cannot discover on the resume and, in turn, the candidate should be learning things about the employer that he or she could not otherwise find out. After all, if you have only thirty minutes, why waste time on information that is already published? The information exchanged is more than just factual, and both sides will learn much from what they see of each other, as well. How the candidate looks, speaks, and acts is important to the employer. The employer's attention to the interview and awareness of the candidate's resume, the setting, and the quality of information presented are important to the candidate.

Just as the employer has every right to be disappointed when a prospect is late for the interview, looks unkempt, and seems ill-prepared to answer fairly standard questions, the candidate may be disappointed with an interviewer who isn't ready for the meeting, hasn't learned the basic resume facts, and is constantly interrupted for telephone calls. In either situation there's good reason to feel let down.

There are many elements to a successful interview, and some of them are not easy to describe or prepare for. Sometimes there is just a chemistry between interviewer and interviewee that brings out the best in both, and a good exchange takes place. But there is much the candidate can do to pave the way for success in terms of his or her resume, personal appearance, goals, and interview strategy—each of which we will discuss. However, none of this preparation is as important as the time and thought the candidate gives to personal self-assessment.

Self-Assessment

Neither a stunning resume nor an expensive, well-tailored suit can compensate for candidates who do not know what they want, where they are going, or why they are interviewing with a particular employer. Self-assessment, the process by which we begin to know and acknowledge our own particular blend of education, experiences, needs, and goals, is not something that can be sorted out the weekend before a major interview. Of all the elements of interview preparation, this one requires the longest lead time and cannot be faked.

Because the time allotted for most interviews is brief, it is all the more important for job candidates to understand and express succinctly why they are there and what they have to offer. This is not a time for undue modesty (or for braggadocio either); but it is a time for a compelling, reasoned statement of why you feel that you and this employer might make a good match. It means you have to have thought about your skills, interests, and attributes; related those to your life experiences and your own history of challenges and opportunities; and determined what that indicates about your strengths, preferences, values, and areas needing further development.

A common complaint of employers is that many candidates didn't take advantage of the interview time, didn't seem to know why they were there or what they wanted. When candidates are asked to talk about themselves and their work-related skills and attributes, employers don't want to be faced with shyness or embarrassed laughter; they need to know about you so they can make a fair determination of you and your competition. If you lose the opportunity to make a case for your employability, you can be certain the person ahead of you has or the person after you will, and it will be on the strength of those impressions that the employer will hire.

If you need some assistance with self-assessment issues, refer to Chapter 1. Included are suggested exercises that can be done as needed, such as making up an experiential diary and extracting obvious strengths and weaknesses from past experiences. These simple, pen-and-paper assignments will help you look at past activities as collections of tasks with accompanying skills and responsibilities. Don't overlook your high school or college career office. Many offer personal counseling on self-assessment issues and may provide testing instruments such as the Myers-Briggs Type Indicator (MBTI)®, the Harrington-O'Shea Career Decision Making® System (CDM), the Strong Interest Inventory (SII)®, or any of a wide selection of assessment tools that can help you clarify some of these issues prior to the interview stage of your job search.

The Resume

Resume preparation has been discussed in detail, and some basic examples of various types were provided. In this section we want to concentrate on how best to use your resume in the interview. In most cases the employer will have seen the resume prior to the interview, and, in fact, it may well have been the quality of that resume that secured the interview opportunity.

An interview is a conversation, however, and not an exercise in reading. So, if the employer hasn't seen your resume and you have brought it along to the interview, wait until asked or until the end of the interview to offer it. Otherwise, you may find yourself staring at the back of your resume and simply answering "yes" and "no" to a series of questions drawn from that document.

Sometimes an interviewer is not prepared and does not know or recall the contents of the resume and may use the resume to a greater or lesser degree as a "prompt" during the interview. It is for you to judge what that may indicate about the individual doing the interview or the employer. If your interviewer seems surprised by the scheduled meeting, relies on the resume to an inordinate degree, and seems otherwise unfamiliar with your background, this lack of preparation for the hiring process could well be a symptom of general management disorganization or may simply be the result of poor planning on the part of one individual. It is your responsibility as a potential employee to be aware of these signals and make your decisions accordingly.

∙∙∙

In any event, it is perfectly acceptable for you to get the conversation back to a more interpersonal style by saying something like "Mr. Smith, you might be interested in some recent experience I gained in an internship that is not detailed on my resume. May I tell you about it?" This can return the interview to two people talking to each other, not one reading and the other responding.

∙∙∙

By all means, bring at least one copy of your resume to the interview. Occasionally, at the close of an interview, an interviewer will express an interest in circulating a resume to several departments, and you could then offer to provide those. Sometimes an interview appointment provides an opportunity to meet others in the organization who may express an interest in you and your background, and it may be helpful to follow that up with a copy of your resume. Our best advice, however, is to keep it out of sight until needed or requested.

Appearance

Although many of the absolute rules that once dominated the advice offered to job candidates about appearance have now been moderated significantly, conservative is still the watchword unless you are interviewing in a fashion-related industry. For men, conservative translates into a well-cut dark suit with appropriate tie, hosiery, and dress shirt. A wise strategy for the male job seeker looking for a good but not expensive suit would be to try the men's department of a major department store. They usually carry a good range of sizes, fabrics, and prices; offer professional sales help; provide free tailoring; and have associated departments for putting together a professional look.

For women, there is more latitude. Business suits are still popular, but they have become more feminine in color and styling with a variety of jacket and skirt lengths. In addition to suits, better-quality dresses are now worn in many environments and, with the correct accessories, can be most appropriate. Company literature, professional magazines, the business section of major newspapers, and television interviews can all give clues about what is being worn in different employer environments.

Both men and women need to pay attention to issues such as hair, jewelry, and makeup; these are often what separates the candidate in appearance from the professional work force. It seems particularly difficult for the young job seeker to give up certain hair styles, eyeglass fashions, and jewelry habits, yet those can be important to the employer, who is concerned with your ability to successfully make the transition into the organization. Candidates often find the best strategy is to dress conservatively until they find employment. Once employed and familiar with the norms within your organization, you can begin to determine a look that you enjoy, works for you, and fits your organization.

Choose clothes that suit your body type, fit well, and flatter you. Feel good about the way you look! The interview day is not the best for a new hairdo, a new pair of shoes, or any other change that will distract you or cause you to be self-conscious. Arrive a bit early to avoid being rushed, and ask the receptionist to direct you to a restroom for any last-minute adjustments of hair and clothes.

Employer Information

Whether your interview is for graduate school admission, an overseas corporate position, or a reporter position with a local newspaper, it is important to know something about the employer or the organization. Keeping in mind that the interview is relatively brief and that you will hopefully have other interviews with other organizations, it is important to keep your research in proportion. If secondary interviews are called for, you will have additional time to do further research. For the first interview, it is helpful to know the organization's mission, goals, size, scope of operations, etc. Your research may uncover recent areas of challenge or particular successes that may help to fuel the interview. Use the "Where Are These Jobs, Anyway?" section of Chapter 3, your library, and your career or guidance office to help you locate this information in the most efficient way possible. Don't be shy in asking advice of these counseling and guidance professionals on how best to spend your preparation time. With some practice, you'll soon learn how much information is enough and which kinds of information are most useful to you.

INTERVIEW CONTENT

We've already discussed how it can help to think of the interview as an important conversation—one that, as with any conversation, you want to find pleasant and interesting and to leave you with a good feeling. But because this conversation is especially important, the information that's exchanged is critical to its success. What do you want them to know about you? What do you need to know about them? What interview technique do you need to particularly pay attention to? How do you want to manage the close of the interview? What steps will follow in the hiring process?

Except for the professional interviewer, most of us find interviewing stressful and anxiety-provoking. Developing a strategy before you begin interviewing will help you relieve some stress and anxiety. One particular strategy that has worked for many and may work for you is interviewing by objective. Before you interview, write down three to five goals you would like to achieve for that interview. They may be technique goals: smile a little more, have a firmer handshake, be sure to ask about the next stage in the interview process before leaving, etc. They may be content-oriented goals: find out about the company's current challenges and opportunities, be sure to speak of my recent research writing experiences or foreign travel, etc. Whatever your goals, jot down a few of them as goals for this interview.

Most people find that, in trying to achieve these few goals, their interviewing technique becomes more organized and focused. After the interview, the most common question friends and family ask is "How did it go?" With this technique, you have an indication of whether you met *your* goals for the meeting, not just some vague idea of how it went. Chances are, if you accomplished what you wanted to, it informed the quality of the entire interview. As you continue to interview, you will want to revise your goals to continue improving your interview skills.

Now, add to the concept of the significant conversation the idea of a beginning, a middle, and a closing and you will have two thoughts that will give your interview a distinctive character. Be sure to make your introduction warm and cordial. Say your full name (and if it's a difficult-to-pronounce name, help the interviewer to pronounce it) and make certain you know your interviewer's name and how to pronounce it. Most interviews begin with some "soft talk" about the weather, chat about the candidate's trip to the interview site, national events, etc. This is done as a courtesy to relax both you and the interviewer, to get you talking, and to generally try to defuse the atmosphere of excessive tension. Try to be yourself, engage in the conversation, and don't try to second-guess the interviewer. This is simply what it appears to be—casual conversation.

Once you and the interviewer move on to exchange more serious information in the middle part of the interview, the two most important concerns become your ability to handle challenging questions and your success at asking meaningful ones. Interviewer questions will probably fall into one of three categories: personal assessment and career direction, academic background, and knowledge of the employer. The following are some examples of questions in each category:

Personal Assessment and Career Direction

1. How would you describe yourself?

2. What motivates you to put forth your greatest effort?

3. In what kind of work environment are you most comfortable?

4. What do you consider to be your greatest strengths and weaknesses?

5. How well do you work under pressure?

6. What qualifications do you have that make you think you will be successful in this career?

7. Will you relocate? What do you feel would be the most difficult aspect of relocating?

8. Are you willing to travel?

9. Why should I hire you?

Academic Assessment

1. Why did you select your college or university?

2. What changes would you make at your alma mater?

3. What led you to choose your major?

4. What subjects did you like best and least? Why?

5. If you could, how would you plan your academic study differently? Why?

6. Describe your most rewarding college experience.

7. How has your college experience prepared you for this career?

8. Do you think that your grades are a good indication of your ability to succeed with this organization?

9. Do you have plans for continued study?

Knowledge of the Employer

1. If you were hiring a graduate of your school for this position, what qualities would you look for?

2. What do you think it takes to be successful in an organization like ours?

3. In what ways do you think you can make a contribution to our organization?

4. Why did you choose to seek a position with this organization?

The interviewer wants a response to each question but is also gauging your enthusiasm, preparedness, and willingness to communicate. In each response you should provide some information about yourself that can be related to the employer's needs. A common mistake is to give too much information. Answer each question completely, but be careful not to run on too long with extensive details or examples.

Questions About Underdeveloped Skills

Most employers interview people who have met some minimum criteria of education and experience. They interview candidates to see who they are, to learn what kind of personality they exhibit, and to get some sense of how this person might fit into the existing organization. It may be that you are asked about skills the employer hopes to find and that you have not documented. Maybe it's grant-writing experience, knowledge of the European political system, or a knowledge of the film world.

To questions about skills and experiences you don't have, answer honestly and forthrightly and try to offer some additional information about skills you do have. For example, perhaps the employer is disappointed you have no grant-writing experience. An honest answer may be as follows:

> No, unfortunately, I was never in a position to acquire those skills. I do understand something of the complexities of the grant-writing process and feel confident that my attention to detail, careful reading skills, and strong writing would make grants a wonderful challenge in a new job. I think I could get up on the learning curve quickly.

The employer hears an honest admission of lack of experience but is reassured by some specific skill details that do relate to grant writing and a confident manner that suggests enthusiasm and interest in a challenge.

For many students questions about their possible contribution to an employer's organization can prove challenging. Because your education has probably not included specific training for a job, you need to review your academic record and select capabilities you have developed in your major that an employer can appreciate. For example, perhaps you read well and can analyze and condense what you've read into smaller, more focused pieces. That could be valuable. Or maybe you did some serious research and you know you have valuable investigative skills. Your public speaking might be highly developed and you might use visual aids appropriately and effectively. Or maybe your skill at correspondence, memos, and messages is effective. Whatever it is, you must take it out of the academic context and put it into a new, employer-friendly context so your interviewer can best judge how you could help the organization.

Exhibiting knowledge of the organization will, without a doubt, show the interviewer that you are interested enough in the available position to have done some legwork in preparation for the interview. Remember, it is not necessary to know every detail of the organization's history, but rather to have a general knowledge about why it is in business and how the industry is faring.

Sometime during the interview, generally after the midway point, you'll be asked if you have any questions for the interviewer. Your questions will tell the employer much about your attitude and your desire to understand the organization's expectations so you can compare it to your own strengths. The following are some selected questions you might want to ask:

1. What are the main responsibilities of the position?

2. What are the opportunities and challenges associated with this position?

3. Could you outline some possible career paths beginning with this position?

4. How regularly do performance evaluations occur?

5. What is the communication style of the organization? (meetings, memos, etc.)

6. Describe a typical day for me in this position.

7. What kinds of opportunities might exist for me to improve my professional skills within the organization?

8. What have been some of the interesting challenges and opportunities your organization has recently faced?

Most interviews draw to a natural closing point, so be careful not to prolong the discussion. At a signal from the interviewer, wind up your presentation, express your appreciation for the opportunity, and be sure to ask what the next stage in the process will be. When can you expect to hear from them?

Will they be conducting second-tier interviews? If you're interested and haven't heard, would they mind a phone call? Be sure to collect a business card with the name and phone number of your interviewer. On your way out, you might have an opportunity to pick up organizational literature you haven't seen before.

With the right preparation—a thorough self-assessment, professional clothing, and employer information—you'll be able to set and achieve the goals you have established for the interview process.

CHAPTER SIX

NETWORKING OR INTERVIEWING FOLLOW-UP

uite often there is a considerable time lag between interviewing for a position and being hired, or, in the case of the networker, between your phone call or letter to a possible contact and the opportunity of a meeting. This can be frustrating. "Why aren't they contacting me?" "I thought I'd get another interview, but no one has telephoned." "Am I out of the running?" You don't know what is happening.

CONSIDER THE DIFFERING PERSPECTIVES

Of course, there is another perspective—that of the networker or hiring organization. Organizations are complex with multiple tasks that need to be accomplished each day. Hiring is but one discrete activity that does not occur as frequently as other job assignments. The hiring process might have to take second place to other, more immediate organizational needs. Although it may be very important to you and it is certainly ultimately significant to the employer, other issues such as fiscal management, planning and product development, employer vacation periods, or financial constraints, may prevent an organization or individual within that organization from acting on your employment or your request for information as quickly as you or they would prefer.

USE YOUR COMMUNICATION SKILLS

Good communication is essential here to resolve any anxieties, and the responsibility is on you, the job or information seeker. Too many job seekers and networkers offer as an excuse that they don't want to "bother" the organization by writing letters or calling. Let us assure you here and now, once and for all, that if you are troubling an organization by over-communicating, someone will indicate that situation to you quite clearly. If not, you can only assume you are a worthwhile prospect and the employer appreciates being reminded of your availability and interest in them. Let's look at follow-up practices in both the job interview process and the networking situation separately.

FOLLOWING UP ON THE EMPLOYMENT INTERVIEW

A brief thank-you note following an interview is an excellent and polite way to begin a series of follow-up communications with a potential employer with whom you have interviewed and want to remain in touch. It should be just that—a thank you for a good meeting. If you failed to mention some fact or experience during your interview that you think might add to your candidacy, you may use this note to do that. However, this should be essentially a note whose overall tone is appreciative and, if appropriate, indicative of a continuing interest in pursuing any opportunity that may exist with that organization. It is one of the few pieces of business correspondence that may be handwritten, but always use plain, good quality, monarch-size paper.

If, however, at this point you are no longer interested in the employer, the thank-you note is an appropriate time to indicate that. You are under no obligation to identify any reason for not continuing to pursue employment with that organization, but if you are so inclined to indicate your professional reasons (pursuing other employers more akin to your interests, looking for greater income production than this employer can provide, a different geographic location than is available, etc.), you certainly may. It should not be written with an eye to negotiation for it will not be interpreted as such.

As part of your interview closing, you should have taken the initiative to establish lines of communication for continuing information about your candidacy. If you asked permission to telephone, wait a week following your thank-you note, then telephone your contact simply to inquire how things are progressing on your employment status. The feedback you receive here should be taken at face value. If your interviewer simply has no information, he or she will tell you so and indicate whether you should call again and when. Don't be discouraged if this should continue over some period of time.

If during this time something occurs that you think improves or changes your candidacy (some new qualification or experience you may have had), including any offers from other organizations, by all means telephone or write to inform the employer about this. In the case of an offer from a competing but less desirable or equally desirable organization, telephone your contact, explain what has happened, express your real interest in the organization, and inquire whether some determination on your employment might be made before you must respond to this other offer. If the organization is truly interested in you, they may be moved to make a decision about your candidacy. Equally possible is the scenario in which they are not yet ready to make a decision and so advise you to take the offer that has been presented. Again, you have no ethical alternative but to deal with the information presented in a straightforward manner.

When accepting other employment, be sure to contact any employers still actively considering you and inform them of your new job. Thank them graciously for their consideration. There are many other job seekers out there just like you who will benefit from having their candidacy improved when others bow out of the race. Who knows, you might at some future time have occasion to interact professionally with one of the organizations with whom you sought employment. How embarrassing to have someone remember you as the candidate who failed to notify them of taking a job elsewhere!

In all of your follow-up communications, keep good notes of who you spoke with, when you called, and any instructions that were given about return communications. This will prevent any misunderstandings and provide you with good records of what has transpired.

FOLLOWING UP ON THE NETWORK CONTACT

Far more common than the forgotten follow-up after an interview is the situation where a good network contact is allowed to lapse. Good communications are the essence of a network, and follow-up is not so much a matter of courtesy here as it is a necessity. In networking for job information and contacts, you are the active network link. Without you, and without continual contact from you, there is no network. You and your need for employment is often the only shared element between members of the network. Because network contacts were made regardless of the availability of any particular employment, it is incumbent upon the job seeker, if not simple common sense, that unless you stay in regular communication with the network, you will not be available for consideration should some job become available in the future.

This brings up the issue of responsibility, which is likewise very clear. The job seeker initiates network contacts and is responsible for maintaining those contacts; therefore, the entire responsibility for the network belongs with him or her. This becomes patently obvious if the network is left unattended. It very shortly falls out of existence because it cannot survive without careful attention by the networker.

A variety of ways are open to you to keep the lines of communication open and to attempt to interest the network in you as a possible employee. You are limited only by your own enthusiasm for members of the network and your creativity. However, you as a networker are well advised to keep good records of whom you have met and spoken with in each organization. Be sure to send thank-you notes to anyone who has spent any time with you, be it a quick tour of a department or a sit-down informational interview. All of these communications should, in addition to their ostensible reason, add some information about you and your particular combination of strengths and attributes.

You can contact your network at any time to convey continued interest, to comment on some recent article you came across concerning an organization, to add information about your training or changes in your qualifications, to ask advice or seek guidance in your job search, or to request referrals to other possible network opportunities. Sometimes just a simple note to network members reminding them of your job search, indicating that you have been using their advice, and noting that you are still actively pursuing leads and hope to continue to interact with them is enough to keep communications alive.

Because networks have been abused in the past, it's important that your conduct be above reproach. Networks are exploratory options, they are not back-door access to employers. The network works best for someone who is exploring a new industry or making a transition into a new area of employment and who needs to find information or to alert people to his or her search activity. Always be candid and direct with contacts in expressing the purpose of your call or letter and your interest in their help or information about their organization. In follow-up contacts keep the tone professional and direct. Your honesty will be appreciated, and people will respond as best they can if your qualifications appear to meet their forthcoming needs. The network does not owe you anything, and that tone should be clear to each person you meet.

FEEDBACK FROM FOLLOW-UPS

A network contact may prove to be miscalculated. Perhaps you were referred to someone and it became clear that your goals and his or her particular needs did not make a good match. Or the network contact may simply not be in a position to provide you with the information you are seeking. Or in some unfortunate situations, the contact may become annoyed by being contacted for this purpose. In such a situation, many job seekers simply say "Thank you" and move on.

If the contact is simply not the right contact, but the individual you are speaking with is not annoyed by the call, it might be a better tactic to express regret that the contact was misplaced and then express to the contact what you are seeking and ask for his or her advice or possible suggestions as to a next step. The more people who are aware you are seeking employment, the better your chances of connecting, and that is the purpose of a network. Most people in a profession have excellent knowledge of their field and varying amounts of expertise on areas near to or tangent to their own. Use their expertise and seek some guidance before you dissolve the contact. You may be pleasantly surprised.

Occasionally, networkers will express the feeling that they have done as much as they can or provided all the information that is available to them. This may be a cue that they would like to be released from your network. Be alert to such attempts to terminate, graciously thank the individual by letter, and move on in your network development. A network is always changing, adding and losing members, and you want the network to be composed only of those who are actively interested in supporting your interests.

A FINAL POINT ON NETWORKING FOR POLITICAL SCIENCE MAJORS

In any field a political science major might consider as a potential career path, your contacts will be critically evaluating all your written and oral communications. For some job seekers this may be more crucial than others. Many of the jobs in the career paths that follow do, however, emphasize communication skills. This should be a welcome demand. Your study of political science has involved writing essays, research papers, and some classroom presentations—all of which have helped polish your communication style.

In your telephone communications, interview presentations, and follow-up correspondence, your written and spoken use of English will be part of the portfolio of impressions you create in those you meet along the way.

CHAPTER SEVEN

JOB OFFER CONSIDERATIONS

or many recent college graduates, the thrill of their first job and, for some, the most substantial regular income they have ever earned seems an excess of good fortune coming at once. To question that first income or be critical in any way of the conditions of employment at the time of the initial offer seems like looking a gift horse in the mouth. It doesn't seem to occur to many new hires even to attempt to negotiate any aspect of their first job. And, as many employers who deal with entry-level jobs for recent college graduates will readily confirm, the reality is that there simply isn't much movement in salary available to these new college recruits. The entry-level hire generally does not have an employment track record on a professional level to provide any leverage for negotiation. Real negotiations on salary, benefits, retirement provisions, etc., come to those with significant employment records at higher income levels.

Of course, the job offer is more than just money. It can be comprised of geographic assignment, duties and responsibilities, training, benefits, health and medical insurance, educational assistance, car allowance or company vehicle, and a host of other items. All of this is generally detailed in the formal letter that presents the final job offer. In most cases this is a follow-up to a personal phone call from the employer representative who has been principally responsible for your hiring process.

That initial telephone offer is certainly binding as a verbal agreement, but most firms follow up with a detailed letter outlining the most significant parts of your employment contract. You may certainly choose to respond immediately at the time of the telephone offer (which would be considered a binding oral contract), but you will also be required to formally answer the letter of offer with a letter of acceptance, restating the salient elements of the employer's description of your position, salary, and benefits. This ensures that both parties are clear on the terms and conditions of employment and remuneration and any other outstanding aspects of the job offer.

IS THIS THE JOB YOU WANT?

Most new employees will write this letter of acceptance back, glad to be in the position to accept employment. If you've worked hard to get the offer and the job market is tight, other offers may not be in sight, so you will say "Yes, I accept!" What is important here is that the job offer you accept be one that does fit your particular needs, values, and interests as you've outlined them in your self-assessment process. Moreover, it should be a job that will not only use your skills and education, but also challenge you to develop new skills and talents.

Jobs are sometimes accepted too hastily, for the wrong reasons, and without proper scrutiny by the applicant. For example, an individual might readily accept a sales job only to find the continual rejection by potential clients unendurable. An office worker might realize within weeks the constraints of a desk job and yearn for more activity. Employment is an important part of our lives. It is, for most of our adult lives, our most continuous productive activity. We want to make good choices based on the right criteria.

If you have a low tolerance for risk, a job based on commission will certainly be very anxiety provoking. If being near your family is important, issues of relocation could present a decision crisis for you. If you're an adventurous person, a job with frequent travel would provide needed excitement and be very desirable. The importance of income, the need to continue your education, your personal health situation—all of these have an impact on whether the job you are considering will ultimately meet your needs. Unless you've spent some time understanding and thinking about these issues, it will be difficult to evaluate offers you do receive.

More importantly, if you make a decision that you cannot tolerate and feel you must leave that job, you will then have both unemployment and self-esteem issues to contend with. These will combine to make the next job search tough going, indeed. So make your acceptance a carefully considered decision.

NEGOTIATING YOUR OFFER

It may be that there is some aspect of your job offer that is not particularly attractive to you. Perhaps there is no relocation allotment to help you move your possessions, and this presents some financial hardship for you. It may be that the medical and health insurance is less than you had hoped. Your initial assignment may be different than you expected, either in its location or in the duties and responsibilities that comprise it. Or it may simply be that the salary is less than you anticipated. Other considerations may be your official starting date of employment, vacation time, evening hours, dates of training programs or schools, etc.

If you are considering not accepting the job because of some item or items in the job offer "package" that do not meet your needs, you should know that most employers emphatically wish that you would bring that issue to their attention. It may be that the employer can alter it to make the offer more agreeable for you. In some cases it cannot be changed. In any event the employer would generally like to have the opportunity to try to remedy a difficulty rather than risk losing a good potential employee over an issue that might have been resolved. After all, they have spent time and funds in securing your services, and they certainly deserve an opportunity to resolve any possible differences.

Honesty is the best approach in discussing any objections or uneasiness you might have over the employer's offer. Having received your formal offer in writing, contact your employer representative and indicate your particular dissatisfaction in a straightforward manner. For example, you might explain that, while very interested in being employed by this organization, the salary (or any other benefit) is less than you have determined you require. State the terms you do need, and listen to the response. You may be asked to put this in writing, or you may be asked to hold off until the firm can decide on a response. If you are dealing with a senior representative of the organization, one who has been involved in hiring for some time, you may get an immediate response or a solid indication of possible outcomes.

Perhaps the issue is one of relocation. Your initial assignment is in the Midwest, and because you had indicated a strong West Coast preference, you are surprised at the actual assignment. You might simply indicate that, while you understand the need for the company to assign you based on its needs, you are disappointed and had hoped to be placed on the West Coast. You could inquire if that were still possible and, if not, would it be reasonable to expect a West Coast relocation in the future.

If your request is presented in a reasonable way, most employers will not see this as jeopardizing your offer. If they can agree to your proposal, they will. If not, they will simply tell you so, and you may choose to continue your candidacy with them or remove yourself from consideration as a possible employee. The choice will be up to you.

Some firms will adjust benefits within their parameters to meet the candidate's need if at all possible. If a candidate requires a relocation cost allowance, he or she may be asked to forgo tuition benefits for the first year to accomplish this adjustment. An increase in life insurance may be adjusted by some other benefit trade-off; perhaps a family dental plan is not needed. In these decisions you are called upon, sometimes under time pressure, to know how you value these issues and how important each is to you.

Many employers find they are more comfortable negotiating for candidates who have unique qualifications or who bring especially needed expertise to the organization. Employers hiring large numbers of entry-level college graduates may be far more reluctant to accommodate any changes in offer conditions. They are well supplied with candidates with similar education and experience, so that if rejected by one candidate, they can draw new candidates from an ample labor pool.

COMPARING OFFERS

With only about 40 percent of recent college graduates employed three months after graduation, many graduates do not get to enjoy the experience of entertaining more than one offer at a time. The conditions of the economy, the job seekers' particular geographic job market, and their own needs and demands for certain employment conditions may not provide more than one offer at a time. Some job seekers may feel that no reasonable offer should go unaccepted for the simple fear there won't be another.

In a tough job market, or if the job you seek is not widely available, or when your job search goes on too long and becomes difficult to sustain financially and emotionally, it may be necessary to accept an offer. The alternative is continued unemployment. Even here, when you feel you don't have a choice, you can at least understand that in accepting this particular offer, there may be limitations and conditions you don't appreciate. At the time of acceptance, there were no other alternatives, but the new employee can begin to use that position to gain the experience and talent to move toward a more attractive position.

Sometimes, however, more than one offer is received at one time, and the candidate has the luxury of choice. If the job seeker knows what he or she wants and has done the necessary self-assessment honestly and thoroughly, it may be clear that one of the offers conforms more closely to those expressed wants and needs.

However, if, as so often happens, the offers are similar in terms of conditions and salary, the question then becomes which organization might provide the necessary climate, opportunities, and advantages for your professional development and growth. This is the time when solid employer research and astute questioning during the interviews really pays off. How much did you learn about the employer through your own research and skillful questioning?

When the interviewer asked during the interview "Do you have any questions?" did you ask the kinds of questions that would help resolve a choice between one organization and another? Just as an employer must decide among numerous applicants, so must the applicant learn to assess the potential employer. Both are partners in the job search.

RENEGING ON AN OFFER

An especially disturbing occurrence for employers and career counseling professionals is when a job seeker formally (either orally or by written contract) accepts employment with one organization and later reneges on the agreement and goes with another employer.

There are all kinds of rationalizations offered for this unethical behavior. None of them satisfies. The sad irony is that what the job seeker is willing to do to the employer—make a promise and then break it—he or she would be outraged to have done to them—have the job offer pulled. It is a very bad way to begin a career. It suggests the individual has not taken the time to do the necessary self-assessment and self-awareness exercises to think and judge critically. The new offer taken may, in fact, be no better or worse than the one refused. Job candidates should be aware that there have been incidents of legal action following job candidates reneging on an offer. This adds a very sour note to what should be a harmonious beginning of a lifelong adventure.

CHAPTER EIGHT

THE GRADUATE SCHOOL CHOICE

The reasons for continuing one's education in graduate school can be as varied and unique as the individuals electing this course of action. Many continue their studies at an advanced level because they simply find it difficult to end the educational process. They love what they are learning and want to learn more and continue their academic exploration.

Continuing to work with a particular subject, such as the dynamics of electoral politics in an increasingly diverse society, and thinking, studying, and writing can provide excitement, challenge, and serious work. Some political science majors have loved this aspect of their academic work and want to continue that activity.

Others go on to graduate school for purely practical reasons. They have examined employment prospects in their field of study and all indications are that a graduate degree is required. You sense opportunities to work at the level you prefer in government, business, or the nonprofit sector would be limited without a master's.

Alumni who are working in the fields you are considering can be a good source of what degree level the field demands. Ask your college career office for some alumni names and give them a telephone call. Prepare some questions on specific job prospects in their field at each degree level. A thorough examination of the marketplace and talking to employers and professors will give you a sense of the scope of employment for a bachelor's, master's, or doctoral degree.

College teaching will require an advanced degree. The more senior executive positions in the career paths outlined in this book will require advanced education and perhaps some particular specialization in a subject area (state legislative processes, constitutional law, etc.).

··

CONSIDER YOUR MOTIVES

The answer to the question of "Why graduate school?" is a personal one for each applicant. Nevertheless, it is important to consider your motives carefully. Graduate school involves additional time out of the employment market, a high degree of critical evaluation, significant autonomy as you pursue your studies, and considerable financial expenditure. For some students in doctoral programs, there may be additional life choice issues, such as relationships, marriage, and parenthood, that may present real challenges while in a program of study. You would be well-advised to consider the following questions as you think about your decision to continue your studies.

Are You Postponing Some Tough Decisions by Going to School?

Graduate school is not a place to go to avoid life's problems. There is intense competition for graduate school slots and for the fellowships, scholarships, and financial aid available. This competition means extensive interviewing, resume submission, and essay writing that rivals corporate recruitment. Likewise, the graduate school process is a mentored one in which faculty stay aware of and involved in the academic progress of their students and continually challenge the quality of their work. Many graduate students are called upon to participate in teaching and professional writing and research as well.

In other words, this is no place to hide from the spotlight. Graduate students work very hard and much is demanded of them individually. If you elect to go to graduate school to avoid the stresses and strains of the "real world," you will find no safe place in higher academics. Vivid accounts, both fiction and nonfiction, have depicted quite accurately the personal and professional demands of graduate school work.

The selection of graduate studies as a career option should be a positive choice—something you *want* to do. It shouldn't be selected as an escape from other, less attractive or more challenging options, nor should it be selected as the option of last resort (i.e., "I can't do anything else; I'd better just stay in school."). If you're in some doubt about the strength of your reasoning about continuing in school, discuss the issues with a career counselor. Together you can clarify your reasoning, and you'll get some sound feedback on what you're about to undertake.

On the other hand, staying on in graduate school because of a particularly poor employment market and a lack of jobs at entry-level positions has proven to be an effective "stalling" strategy. If you can afford it, pursuing a graduate degree immediately after your undergraduate education gives you a year or two to "wait out" a difficult economic climate while at the same time acquiring a potentially valuable credential.

Have You Done Some "Hands-On" Reality Testing?

There are experiential options available to give some reality to your decision-making process about graduate school. Internships or work in the field can give you a good idea about employment demands, conditions, and atmosphere.

· ·

A master's degree is the frequent choice of political science majors who hope to advance their careers. You'll want to read Chapters Ten through Thirteen in this book to understand how you can make the most of both your graduate education and your career. Publications such as *The Chronicle of Higher Education* contain articles that can provide background information on graduate studies and their applications.

For political science majors who want to take their graduate education to the doctoral level with an eye to college teaching or research, the need for some "hands-on" reality testing is vital. Begin with your own college professors and ask them to talk to you about their own educational and career paths that have taken them to their current teaching posts. They will have had actual experience and will have inside information regarding the current market for Ph.D.s in political science.

> Whether it's a master's or a Ph.D. in political science that is in your future, the kind of reality tests that come through internships, part-time jobs, and, most importantly, talking to people who have attained the kinds of careers you are seeking will give you the best kind of information to make your decision.

....

Do You Need an Advanced Degree to Work in Your Field?

Certainly there are fields such as law, psychiatry, medicine, and college teaching that demand advanced degrees. Is the field of employment you're considering one that also puts a premium on an advanced degree? You may be surprised. Read the want ads in a number of major Sunday newspapers for positions you would enjoy. How many of those require an advanced degree?

Retailing, for example, has always put a premium on what people can do, rather than how much education they have had. Successful people in retailing come from all academic preparations. A Ph.D. in English may bring only prestige to the individual employed as a magazine researcher. It may not bring a more senior position or better pay. In fact, it may disqualify you for some jobs because an employer might believe you will be unhappy to be overqualified for a particular position. Or your motives in applying for the work may be misconstrued, and the employer might think you will only be working at this level until something better comes along. None of this may be true for you, but it comes about because you are working outside of the usual territory for that degree level.

When economic times are especially difficult, we tend to see stories featured about individuals with advanced degrees doing what is considered unsuitable work, such as the Ph.D. in English driving a cab or the Ph.D. in chemistry waiting tables. Actually, this is not particularly surprising when you consider that as your degree level advances, the job market narrows appreciably. At any one time, regardless of economic circumstances, there are only so many jobs for your particular level of expertise. If you cannot find employment for your advanced degree level, chances are you will be considered suspect for many other kinds of employment and may be forced into temporary work far removed from your original intention.

Before making an important decision such as graduate study, learn your options and carefully consider what you want to do with your advanced degree. Ask yourself whether it is reasonable to think you can achieve your goals. Will there be jobs when you graduate? Where will they be? What will they pay? How competitive will the market be at that time, based on current predictions?

If you're uncertain about the degree requirements for the fields you're interested in, you should check a publication such as the U.S. Department of Labor's *Occupational Outlook Handbook*. Each entry has a section on training and other qualifications that will indicate clearly what the minimum educational requirement is for employment, what degree is the standard, and what employment may be possible without the required credential.

For example, for physicists and astronomers, a doctoral degree in physics or a closely related field is essential. Certainly this is the degree of choice in academic institutions. However, the *Occupational Outlook Handbook* also indicates what kinds of employment may be available to individuals holding a master's or even a bachelor's degree in physics.

Have You Compared Your Expectations of What Graduate School Will Do for You with What It Has Done for Alumni of the Program You're Considering?

Most colleges and universities perform some kind of postgraduate survey of their students to ascertain where they are employed, what additional education they have received, and what levels of salary they are enjoying. Ask to see this information either from the university you are considering applying to or from your own alma mater, especially if it has a similar graduate program. Such surveys often reveal surprises about occupational decisions, salaries, and work satisfaction. This information may affect your decision.

The value of self-assessment (the process of examining and making decisions about your own hierarchy of values and goals) is especially important in this process of analyzing the desirability of possible career paths involving graduate education. Sometimes a job requiring advanced education seems to hold real promise but is disappointing in salary potential or number of opportunities available. Certainly it is better to research this information before embarking on a program of graduate studies. It may not change your mind about your decision, but by becoming better informed about your choice, you become better prepared for your future.

Have You Talked with People in Your Field to Explore What You Might Be Doing After Graduate School?

In pursuing your undergraduate degree, you will have come into contact with many individuals trained in the field you are considering. You might also have the opportunity to attend professional conferences, workshops, seminars, and job fairs where you can expand your network of contacts. Talk to them all!

Find out about their individual career paths, discuss your own plans and hopes, and get their feedback on the reality of your expectations, and heed their advice about your prospects. Each will have a unique tale to tell, and each will bring a different perspective on the current marketplace for the credentials you are seeking. Talking to enough people will make you an expert on what's out there.

Are You Excited by the Idea of Studying the Particular Field You Have in Mind?

This question may be the most important one of all. If you are going to spend several years in advanced study, perhaps engendering some debt or postponing some lifestyle decisions for an advanced degree, you simply ought to enjoy what you're doing. Examine your work in the discipline so far. Has it been fun? Have you found yourself exploring various paths of thought? Do you read in your area for fun? Do you enjoy talking about it, thinking about it, and sharing it with others? Advanced degrees often are the beginning of a lifetime's involvement with a particular subject. Choose carefully a field that will hold your interest and your enthusiasm.

It is fairly obvious by now that we think you should give some careful thought to your decision and take some action. If nothing else, do the following:

- Talk and question (remember to listen!)

- Reality-test

- Soul-search by yourself or with a person you trust

FINDING THE RIGHT PROGRAM FOR YOU: SOME CONSIDERATIONS

There are several important factors in coming to a sound decision about the right graduate program for you. You'll want to begin by locating institutions that offer appropriate programs, examining each of these programs and their requirements, undertaking the application process by obtaining catalogs and application materials, visiting campuses if possible, arranging for letters of recommendation, writing your application statement, and finally following up on your applications.

Locate Institutions with Appropriate Programs

Once you decide on a particular advanced degree, it's important to develop a list of schools offering such a degree program. Perhaps the best sources of graduate program information are Peterson's *Guides to Graduate Study.* Use these guides to build your list. In addition, you may want to consult the College Board's *Index of Majors and Graduate Degrees,* which will help you find graduate programs offering the degree you seek. It is indexed by academic major and then categorized by state.

Now, this may be a considerable list. You may want to narrow the choices down further by a number of criteria: tuition, availability of financial aid, public versus private institutions, U.S. versus international institutions, size of student body, size of faculty, application fee (this varies by school; most fall within the $10–$75 range), and geographic location. This is only a partial list; you will have your own important considerations. Perhaps you are an avid scuba diver and you find it unrealistic to think you could pursue graduate study for a number of years without being able to ocean dive from time to time. Good! That's a decision and it's honest. Now, how far from the ocean is too far, and what schools meet your other needs? In any case, and according to your own criteria, begin to build a reasonable list of graduate schools that you are willing to spend the time investigating.

Examine the Degree Programs and Their Requirements

Once you've determined the criteria by which you want to develop a list of graduate schools, you can begin to examine the degree program requirements, faculty composition, and institutional research orientation. Again, using resources such as Peterson's *Guides to Graduate Study* can reveal an amazingly rich level of material by which to judge your possible selections.

In addition to degree programs and degree requirements, entries will include information about application fees, entrance test requirements, tuition, percentage of applicants accepted, numbers of applicants receiving financial aid, gender breakdown of students, numbers of full- and part-time faculty, and often gender breakdown of faculty as well. Numbers graduating in each program and research orientations of departments are also included in some entries. There is information on graduate housing, student services, and library, research, and computer facilities. A contact person, phone number, and address are also standard pieces of information in these listings. In addition to the standard entries, some schools pay an additional fee to place full-page, more detailed program descriptions. The location of such a display ad, if present, would be indicated at the end of the standard entry.

It can be helpful to draw up a chart and enter relevant information about each school you are considering in order to have a ready reference on points of information that are important to you.

Undertake the Application Process

The Catalog. Once you've decided on a selection of schools, send for catalogs and applications. It is important to note here that these materials might take many weeks to arrive. Consequently, if you need the materials quickly, it might be best to telephone and explain your situation to see whether the process can be speeded up for you. Also, check a local college or university library, which might have current and complete college catalogs in a microfiche collection. These microfiche copies can provide you with helpful information while you wait for your own copy of the graduate school catalog or bulletin to arrive.

When you receive your catalogs, give them a careful reading and make notes of issues you might want to discuss on the telephone or in a personal interview, if that's possible. Does the course selection have the depth you had hoped for?

What is the ratio of faculty to the required number of courses for your degree? How often will you encounter the same faculty member as an instructor?

••••••••••••••••••••••••••••••••••••••

If you are interested in graduate work in public administration, for example, in addition to classroom courses in urban planning or management, consider the availability of colloquiums, directed research opportunities, and specialized seminars.

••••••••••••••••••••••••••••••••••••••

If, for example, your program offers a practicum or off-campus experience, who arranges this? Does the graduate school select a site and place you there, or is it your responsibility? What are the professional affiliations of the faculty? Does the program merit any outside professional endorsement or accreditation?

Critically evaluate the catalogs of each of the programs you are considering. List any questions you have and ask current or former teachers and colleagues for their impressions as well.

The Application. Preview each application thoroughly to determine what you need to provide in the way of letters of recommendation, transcripts from undergraduate schools or any previous graduate work, and personal essays that may be required. Make a notation for each application of what you need to complete that document.

Additionally, you'll want to determine entrance testing requirements for each institution and immediately arrange to complete your test registration.

For example, the Graduate Record Exam (GRE) and the Law School Admission Test (LSAT) each have several weeks between the last registration date and the test date. Your local college career office should be able to provide you with test registration booklets, sample test materials, information on test sites and dates, and independent test review materials that might be available commercially.

Visit the Campus If Possible

If time and finances allow, a visit, interview, and tour can help make your decision easier. You can develop a sense of the student body, meet some of the faculty, and hear up-to-date information on resources and the curriculum. You will have a brief opportunity to "try out" the surroundings to see if they fit your needs. After all, it will be home for a while. If a visit is not possible but you have questions, don't hesitate to call and speak with the dean of the graduate school. Most are more than happy to talk to candidates and want them to have the answers they seek. Graduate school admission is a very personal and individual process.

Arrange for Letters of Recommendation

This is also the time to begin to assemble a group of individuals who will support your candidacy as a graduate student by writing letters of recommendation or completing recommendation forms. Some schools will ask you to provide letters of recommendation to be included with your application or sent directly to the school by the recommender. Other graduate programs will provide a recommendation form that must be completed by the recommender. These graduate school forms vary greatly in the amount of space provided for a written recommendation. So that you can use letters as you need to, ask your recommenders to address their letters "To Whom It May Concern," unless one of your recommenders has a particular connection to one of your graduate schools or knows an official at the school.

Choose recommenders who can speak authoritatively about the criteria important to selection officials at your graduate school. In other words, choose recommenders who can write about your grasp of the literature in your field of study, your ability to write and speak effectively, your class performance, and your demonstrated interest in the field outside of class. Other characteristics that graduate schools are interested in assessing include your emotional maturity, leadership ability, breadth of general knowledge, intellectual ability, motivation, perseverance, and ability to engage in independent inquiry.

When requesting recommendations, it's especially helpful to put the request in writing. Explain your graduate school intentions and express some of your thoughts about graduate school and your appreciation for their support. Don't be shy about "prompting" your recommenders with some suggestions of what you would appreciate being included in their comments. Most recommenders will find this direction helpful and will want to produce a statement of support that you can both stand behind. Consequently, if your interaction with one recommender was especially focused on research projects, he or she might be best able to speak of those skills and your critical thinking ability. Another recommender may have good comments to make about your public presentation skills.

Give your recommenders plenty of lead time in which to complete your recommendation, and set a date by which they should respond. If they fail to meet your deadline, be prepared to make a polite call or visit to inquire if they need more information or if there is anything you can do to move the process along.

Whether or not you are providing a graduate school form or asking for an original letter to be mailed, be sure to provide an envelope and postage if the recommender must mail the form or letter directly to the graduate school.

Each recommendation you request should provide a different piece of information about you for the selection committee. It might be pleasant for letters of recommendation to say that you are a fine, upstanding individual, but a selection committee for graduate school will require specific information. Each recommender has had a unique relationship with you, and their letters should reflect that. Think of each letter as helping to build a more complete portrait of you as a potential graduate student.

Write Your Application Statement

> For the political science major, the application and personal essay should be a welcome opportunity to express your deep interest in pursuing graduate study. Your understanding of the challenges ahead, your commitment to the work involved, and your expressed self-awareness will weigh heavily in the decision process of the graduate school admissions committee.

An excellent source to help in thinking about writing this essay is *How to Write a Winning Personal Statement for Graduate and Professional School* by Richard J. Stelzer. It has been written from the perspective of what graduate school selection committees are looking for when they read these essays. It provides helpful tips to keep your essay targeted on the kinds of issues and criteria that are important to selection committees and that provide them with the kind of information they can best utilize in making their decision.

Follow Up on Your Applications

After you have finished each application and mailed it along with your transcript requests and letters of recommendation, be sure to follow up on the progress of your file. For example, call the graduate school administrative staff to see whether your transcripts have arrived. If the school required your recommenders to fill out a specific recommendation form that had to be mailed directly to the school, you will want to ensure that they have all arrived in good time for the processing of your application. It is your responsibility to make certain that all required information is received by the institution.

RESEARCHING FINANCIAL AID SOURCES, SCHOLARSHIPS, AND FELLOWSHIPS

Financial aid information is available from each school, so be sure to request it when you call for a catalog and application materials. There will be several lengthy forms to complete, and these will vary by school, type of school (public versus private), and state. Be sure to note the deadline dates for these important forms.

There are many excellent resources available to help you explore all of your financial aid options. Visit your college career office or local public library to find out about the range of materials available. Two excellent resources include Peterson's *Grants for Graduate Students* and the Foundation Center's *Foundation Grants to Individuals.* These types of resources generally contain information that can be accessed by indexes including field of study, specific eligibility requirements, administering agency, and geographic focus.

EVALUATING ACCEPTANCES

If you apply to and are accepted at more than one school, it is time to return to your initial research and self-assessment to evaluate your options and select the program that will best help you achieve the goals you set for pursuing graduate study. You'll want to choose a program that will allow you to complete your studies in a timely and cost-effective way. This may be a good time to get additional feedback from professors and career professionals who are familiar with your interests and plans. Ultimately, the decision is yours, so be sure you get answers to all the questions you can think of.

SOME NOTES ABOUT REJECTION

Each graduate school is searching for applicants who appear to have the qualifications necessary to succeed in its program. Applications are evaluated on a combination of undergraduate grade point average, strength of letters of recommendation, standardized test scores, and personal statements written for the application.

A carelessly completed application is one reason many applicants are denied admission to a graduate program. To avoid this type of needless rejection, be sure to carefully and completely answer all appropriate questions on the application form, focus your personal statement given the instructions provided, and submit your materials well in advance of the deadline. Remember that your test scores and recommendations are considered a part of your application, so they must also be received by the deadline.

If you are rejected by a school that especially interests you, you may want to contact the dean of graduate studies to discuss the strengths and weaknesses of your application. Information provided by the dean will be useful in reapplying to the program or applying to other, similar programs.

PART TWO

THE CAREER PATHS

CHAPTER NINE

INTRODUCTION TO THE POLITICAL SCIENCE CAREER PATHS

f ifty thousand years ago human beings were largely uncivilized. They hunted animals and gathered fruits and other plant foods, living together in packs or clans. There was no written language and of course, no formal government.

A witty commentator looking at today's political scene might laugh and say, "Those were the good old days!" But the truth is, life without government was not idyllic. As people became civilized and developed villages and cities, the need for government became apparent. Over the centuries it became a fixture of civilized life.

In recent decades academics have studied the processes of government and politics and shaped a respected academic discipline. Political science is a subject studied in great detail by students, researchers, professors, and others.

AREAS OF STUDY IN POLITICAL SCIENCE

In its most basic terms political science consists of the study of politics and government. Within this field students and researchers tend to focus their attention on a few major areas. Following is a description of some of the primary areas of study within the overall field of political science.

National Politics

A major topic in political science is the study of national politics. In the United States this would consist of American or U.S. politics; in Canada it would involve the Canadian political system.

The study of national politics typically includes philosophical foundations of the national-level government, constitutional development, and the various institutions within the government. This would include the major branches of government and how they operate. It would also include contemporary issues related to the electoral process, party politics, and government policies and practices at the national level.

Public Administration

Public administration deals with the practical aspects of managing government operations. It focuses on principles of administration such as planning, budgeting, and supervising. A common goal of public administration is to enhance the operating efficiency of public organizations.

Comparative Politics

In this area comparisons of political processes and governmental organizations are made. This can include analysis of government at various levels. For example, the legislative process in different states might be compared, or the different ways local governments obtain tax revenues might be studied.

International Relations

No country exists in isolation. The interaction between countries is the basis for the study of international relations. Trade agreements, mutual security treaties, economic exchanges, and other affairs among nations provide the basis for an extensive area of study.

Other Areas of Study

Other areas of study range from constitutional law to the history of political parties. The University of Wisconsin has identified the following subfields of possible interest to political science majors:

- Political parties and voting behavior
- Bureaucracies and administrative procedure
- International politics and organization
- Executive politics and legislative behavior

❑ Political socialization and recruitment

❑ Community organization and urban politics

❑ Courts and the administration of justice

❑ Interest groups

❑ Intergovernmental relations

❑ Political personality

❑ Mass movements and revolutions

❑ Political philosophy

❑ Policy studies

ADVANTAGE OF A DEGREE

A bachelor's degree is not always a quick ticket to a challenging job. After all, more people are going to college than ever before, and the shifting nature of the contemporary economy has brought a great deal of uncertainty when it comes to careers.

At the same time, a bachelor's degree is almost always an asset, and with persistence most people who earn a college degree find it advances their occupational choices. Aside from its intrinsic value, a degree can be a major factor in landing a good job. After all, only about 20 percent of American adults hold a bachelor's degree or higher, according to the U.S. Census. That means that four out of five adults in the United States lack a college degree. In seeking employment or in advancing on the job once you're employed, a degree can make the difference.

Political science graduates not only benefit from the general knowledge obtained in completing a liberal arts degree; they also acquire specialized knowledge about governmental systems. Some courses in this field cover broad areas of political philosophy, while others focus on more specific governmental practices. The combined result prepares political science majors to perform a wide range of tasks related to government, law, organizational management, and other areas.

An event sponsored by the University of Minnesota illustrates the diversity of careers open to political science majors. At a recent career day five former graduates of the political science program returned to campus and talked to students about their careers. The five included the Speaker of the Minnesota House of Representatives, a chief legislative aide to a United States senator, a graduate who went on to law school and recently received her law degree from Yale, a businesswoman who develops Web pages for private companies, and a grad who works with the Ordway Music Theatre in St. Paul, Minnesota.

According to University of Minnesota officials, many former graduates work in government. Substantial numbers have gone on to law school. Many of them have used their liberal arts backgrounds to pursue employment in management, the media, as lobbyists, and in other occupations. A similar story can be found for the graduates of almost any college or university offering a major in political science.

Many students who earn a bachelor's degree in political science go on to pursue a master's degree. This is a frequent choice of political science majors who hope to enhance their careers. The graduate degree may be in political science or a more specialized aspect of the field, such as international relations. Or it might be in a completely different field such as public administration, urban planning, business administration, finance, or communications.

Whether they go to graduate school or enter the workforce after completing a bachelor's degree, political science majors end up working in a wide range of career areas. Like any liberal arts field, political science, when combined with the other disciplines studied as part of the general education component of all bachelor's degrees, provides a solid foundation for understanding the world around us and for thinking critically. The tools learned in college, from reading and writing with skill to analyzing and understanding complex information, prepare students to adapt to a variety of workplace needs. In addition, the knowledge gained by political science students, such as how political systems operate and the basic processes of government, can be applied in a host of jobs. From the lobbyist approaching a senator to the judge who interprets the constitutionality of a law introduced by the latter, preparation at the undergraduate level in political science can be the start of an exciting and productive career.

The following chapters cover some of the career paths that can be followed in this field. Listings are not exhaustive, but they should provide a good overview of some of the possibilities that await you. Here are the career paths discussed:

1. Public service

2. Teaching

3. Law

4. Nonprofit management

These paths are offered as realistic suggestions, with the hope they will stimulate your thinking about possible career directions. You will also be able to think of other options. With effort and creativity, you should be able to make a case for your political science degree in any number of job situations.

CHAPTER TEN

PATH 1:
PUBLIC SERVICE

As a political science major, you understand the importance of government. You realize that without government in its various forms, our lives would be vastly different. In fact civilization in its present form would be impossible.

At its very basic levels, government can rely on work contributed by citizens. The original idea behind most state legislatures was that citizens would give a portion of their time to serve in the legislature, but that this would not be their profession. The idea of the part-time legislator is still alive today to some extent. But it has been greatly overshadowed by the growth of a different concept: that of the career public servant. Today we have millions of people who earn their livelihoods as government employees. This includes specialized areas such as teachers, military personnel, and others, but it also includes a large number of managers and professional employees who conduct the work performed by government agencies.

This area represents fertile ground for the political science major. Someone must provide the services demanded by the citizens of a highly structured society. In many cases that someone can be the holder of a degree in political science.

DEFINITION OF THE CAREER PATH

"Public service" is a broad term. To begin to define this term within the context of career planning, here are some basic facts about public service as a career path.

❑ Public service jobs include jobs within various levels of government.

❑ Almost all public service jobs involve working in a noncommercial, nonprofit role. Directly or indirectly, this means serving the public.

❑ Some public service jobs, such as those of state legislators and members of Congress, can only be attained by being elected by the public.

❑ Some public service jobs consist of positions appointed through a formal government process. For certain high-level jobs this means being officially appointed by an executive such as a governor or by a legislative body. For others it means going through a civil service process based on taking examinations or meeting other specific criteria.

❑ Some jobs in public service involve an application process very similar to that of the business world. Instead of being elected or appointed by an official body, applicants go through an interview process and are selected by the supervisor for the position.

❑ The duties of many public service jobs require an understanding of government policies and regulations. Many involve direct work with government agencies.

❑ Some public service careers require very specific skills not normally attained by political science majors (for example, working as an engineer with the U.S. Corps of Engineers). Others involve a general understanding of politics, government, and related matters with which political science majors are quite familiar. These include the career areas on which this book focuses.

POSSIBLE JOB TITLES

The U.S. Department of Labor lists a wide range of job titles in its *Dictionary of Occupational Titles*. Among those classified under "government service" are

Administrative officer	Caseworker
Appeal referee	Civil preparedness officer
Appeals reviewer	Claims adjudicator
Area representative	Commissioner, conservation of resources
Budget analyst	
Business-enterprise officer	County agent

County director, welfare

Court officer

Cultural affairs officer

Customs inspector

Deputy assessor

Diplomatic officer

Director, commission for the blind

Director, compliance

Director, consumer affairs

Director, council on aging

Director, employment research and planning

Director, field representatives

Director, labor standards

Director, licensing and administration

Director, merit system

Director, regulatory agency

Director, revenue

Director, safety council

Director, sanitation council

Director, social services

Director, traffic and planning

Director, unemployment insurance

Director, vital statistics

Economic development coordinator

Economic officer

Election assistant

Election supervisor

Housing management officer

Identification officer

Immigration officer

Information officer

Insurance licensing supervisor

Intelligence specialist

Legislative aide

Legislative assistant

License inspector

Manager, city

Manager, county

Manager for health, safety, and environment

Manager, governmental program

Manager, office

Manager, regulated program

Manager, surplus property

Manager, town

Municipal services supervisor

Occupational-safety-and-health compliance officer

Passport application examiner

Personnel administrator

Personnel recruiter

Political officer

Public works commissioner

Position classifier

Program manager

Prosecuting attorney

Public affairs officer

Public finance specialist

Public utilities complaint analyst
   supervisor

Regional coordinator for aging

Rehabilitation center manager

Reports analyst

Retirement officer

Secretary of state

Special agent

Unclaimed property officer

Urban planner

Welfare director

REPRESENTATIVE PUBLIC SERVICE JOBS

If you want to follow a career path that is directly related to your studies as a political science major, consider serving as a government official. Such jobs include positions in different branches of government at the local, state or provincial, and federal levels. Some, such as state legislators and members of Congress, are elected positions. Others, such as state level cabinet positions, are based on appointments from governors or other officials.

Executive positions involve the various responsibilities of managing government agencies or other governmental units. At the top of this list is the president of the United States. This is a job you may want to pursue, but job openings are few, and the competition is stiff! Other executive positions include governors of states, lieutenant governors, mayors of cities and towns, and county executives. In addition to highly visible elected executives, there are many positions in which an individual is hired by top-level managers, boards, or others to administer the business of an agency, department, or other unit.

Town or City Manager

Most cities and towns (with the exception of very small communities) employ a professional manager. The person in this position is responsible for managing the day-to-day affairs of municipal government.

Responsibilities of this position vary widely. In a large city much of the job involves supervising other managers and staff who take care of specific responsibilities ranging from economic development to collection of utility payments. In a small town more "hands-on" work may be required because the number of other staff is often limited.

Typically, a city manager takes care of the everyday business of the city. He or she manages city employees, runs the municipal offices, and carries out the direction of the city council or other governing body.

Federal Agency Manager

Many of the affairs of government are handled by agencies or similar bodies. For example, the Environmental Protection Agency monitors environmental concerns and implements laws passed by Congress in this area. The Department of Commerce focuses on business concerns. The State Department deals with foreign policy and relations with other nations.

For these and countless other agencies and departments, managers are employed to implement policy, deal with the public, and provide general management oversight. Of course duties vary widely. The Secretary of State who gives a major speech to the United Nations and the junior assistant who clips newspaper articles from foreign newspapers are both employees of the same agency, and both are public servants.

State Agency Manager

Just as the federal government operates a labyrinth of agencies and departments, states and provinces employ their own legions of managers, support staff, and other workers. Jobs of this type range from a state's Director of Public Safety to the human resources managers who hire and evaluate state employees.

Legislative Assistant

Many public service jobs involve staff roles in support of government functions. For example, consider the role of legislative assistant.

Mention the prospect of a career as a legislator, and most people would probably envision serving as a member of the United States Congress or Canada's Parliament. But this is actually a limited point of view. For every elected legislative position at the national level, there are scores of support roles. To a lesser degree this is also true at the state level. Many of these jobs require a solid understanding of the political process, and as such represent job choices worth considering for political science majors.

A legislative assistant works in a career area in which the knowledge gained in studying political science has direct applicability. This includes both federal and state positions.

The United States Congress includes 100 senators and 435 members of the House of Representatives. Each of these elected officials employs a large staff of people assigned to a variety of support roles. In addition, congressional committees and the major parties and other political organizations employ staff. Duties might include writing letters to constituents, developing draft legislation, conducting background research, planning election campaigns, or scheduling meetings with other legislators.

Elected Official

Of course you can also seek elected office. Pick up a newspaper or watch televised news, and you will see plenty of information about the people representing you in government. If you aspire to become one of those representatives, a political science background can help get you started. Such roles include member of the House of Representatives; U.S. senator; state legislator; mayor; governor; attorney general; and others.

POSSIBLE EMPLOYERS

Public service jobs can be found in a wide range of agencies and organizations. The federal government is made up of scores of agencies, departments, commissions, and bureaus. Each state also has its own elaborate governmental structure. City, town, and county governments, as well as regional consortia and other groups, also employ large numbers of personnel.

Here are some possible employers in the public service area. Many more could be listed; these are merely examples.

Agency for International Development

City governments

County governments

Defense Logistics Agency

Department of Agriculture

Department of the Air Force

Department of the Army

Department of Commerce

Department of Defense

Department of Education

Department of Energy

Department of Health and Human Services

Department of Housing and Urban Development

Department of the Interior

Department of Justice

Department of Labor

Department of the Navy

Department of State

Department of Transportation

Department of the Treasury

Department of Veterans Affairs

Environmental Protection Agency

Executive Office of the President

Federal Trade Commission

General Services Administration

National Aeronautics and Space Administration

National Credit Union Administration

National Science Foundation

Nuclear Regulatory Commission

Railroad Retirement Board

Regional planning agencies

State departments of social services

State legislatures

Tennessee Valley Authority

U.S. Information Agency

U.S. Postal Service

Planning Organizations

Most states have several regional or metropolitan planning organizations. These groups conduct activities related to economic development, grant development, regional planning, and other functions.

The following list includes just a few of these organizations.

Green River Area Development District (Kentucky)

Hampton Roads Planning District Commission (Virginia)

Indian River County Metropolitan Planning Organization (Florida)

Merrimac Valley Planning Commission (Massachusetts)

Mid-Ohio Regional Planning Commission

Northeastern Illinois Planning Commission

Rhode Island State Planning Council

Tampa Bay Regional Planning Council (Florida)

WORKING CONDITIONS

Because public service jobs cover so many areas, working conditions may vary markedly. In general, workers in this field enjoy comfortable working environments.

Typically, public service jobs involve a significant amount of office work. The office setting may vary from a tiny, single cubicle to an expansive office with plush furnishings. Often this is an indicator of authority and seniority, with senior executives enjoying offices that are larger and more impressive than those of more junior personnel. But this is by no means a standard practice. Office environments may vary depending on a number of factors: the age of the building in which an office is located; the way in which office space has historically been apportioned within an organization; staffing trends resulting in increases or reductions in the demand for office space; and other considerations.

Regardless of the size or furnishings of an office, it typically includes a few basics such as a desk, chair, telephone, and computer. Related work environments may include conference rooms, offices of coworkers, and large meeting rooms. In addition, many public service jobs require work outside of the office setting. This can also vary widely. A town manager or urban planner may spend time walking through old buildings that have been designated for remodeling and use as part of a new industrial park. An employee of a United States embassy in another country may end up driving through a jungle to check on some American relief workers. A legislator may spend time visiting a constituent's farm one day and making a speech in the state capitol the next.

TRAINING AND QUALIFICATIONS

For public service jobs a bachelor's degree is a good starting point in qualifying for a job. In some cases less than a bachelor's is required, but having a degree can make you more competitive.

With the federal government, holding a bachelor's degree makes you eligible for appointment at the GS-5 level (see section on earnings). You may be able to qualify for positions such as personnel specialist or budget analyst with a degree in any major, including political science.

After completing a bachelor's degree with a major in political science, you might want to pursue a master's degree. An advanced degree can be valuable both in landing new jobs and in advancing once you are employed.

One approach is to combine a bachelor's degree in political science with a master's degree in a different but related field. For example, a master's degree in urban planning can effectively complement a bachelor's with a major in political science. Completion of the second degree can bring enhanced prospects for obtaining certain jobs. Typical positions include that of assistant town manager in a small town, assistant county administrator, or planning officer in a state or regional planning agency.

Many political science graduates find the master's in public administration (MPA) an attractive option. This degree can prepare you to work in diverse fields such as regional planning, city management, nonprofit management, environmental planning, or social services administration.

According to the National Association of Schools of Public Affairs and Administration, over 6,000 graduate degrees in public administration are awarded annually. More than 200 colleges and universities offer programs in this field, and over 26,000 students are enrolled.

Titles of degree offerings vary. Examples include master of public administration, master of public policy, master of public affairs, master of public management, or master of public management and administration.

Course offerings in public administration cover areas such as the following:

- Economics

- Financial management

- Policy analysis

- Public sector institutions

- Legal procedures

- Organization management

- Human resources management

Another option is to seek a master's degree or higher in political science itself. Still another approach is to obtain a master of business administration (MBA) or another degree that involves management.

One advantage of graduate study is that in many cases you can study on a part-time basis while you work full time. Completing 36 credits for a master's degree is much more manageable than earning the 120 credits or more needed for a bachelor's degree.

EARNINGS

Those employed in public service jobs earn a wide range of salaries. Some people complain that in general, government jobs pay less than corresponding jobs in the private sector. But at the same time government employees tend to enjoy more job security. Not only are they protected by well-developed personnel policies, but the reality of life is different than in most private businesses. After all, one company may go out of business or be acquired by another, but who's going to buy the government? Certainly government employees are vulnerable to cutbacks or other problems, but in general they enjoy excellent job security as well as good benefits.

For personnel employed by the federal government, salaries may be established by a highly structured plan known as the General Schedule (GS) plan. Under this system jobs are rated at fifteen different levels based on a combination of job demands and qualifications needed to fill the position. Specific salaries are attached to each level.

For 1998 basic pay under the GS plan was as follows:

GS-1	$12,960	GS-6	$22,258	GS-11	$36,609
GS-2	$14,571	GS-7	$24,734	GS-12	$43,876
GS-3	$15,899	GS-8	$27,393	GS-13	$52,176
GS-4	$17,848	GS-9	$30,257	GS-14	$61,656
GS-5	$19,969	GS-10	$33,320	GS-15	$72,525

These figures represent base salaries, but most jobs actually pay more. The government adjusts GS pay geographically, and when locality payments are included, pay rates within the continental United States may go as much as 12 percent higher. Outside the continental United States, pay rates are 10 to 25 percent higher.

In addition, some starting salaries are higher in hard-to-fill fields. Experienced employees also tend to build up higher salaries as time on the job lengthens.

What if you have a college degree in political science but no directly related job experience? According to the U.S. Office of Personnel Management, you would start out at a GS-5 level. If you maintained a B average or meet other academic credentials, you can start at GS-7. If you have a master's degree directly related to the job in question, you can qualify for a GS-9 rating.

Keep in mind that not all federal government jobs use the GS pay plan. For example, U.S. attorneys and judges have their own pay scales, as do members of Congress and those in a variety of other roles.

At the state and local level salaries vary tremendously from one state to the next or among different branches of government and different departments. To get an idea of salaries for jobs in your city or state, check ads for job openings or consult officials at government agencies in which you are interested.

IDENTIFYING JOB OPENINGS

You can follow a number of strategies to identify job openings in public or government service. One approach is to work through professional associations.

The American Society for Public Administration (ASPA), for example, has a membership of more than 12,000 people. Members include not only those employed in public service, but also teachers and students. Membership in this type of organization can be a valuable resource during the job search process.

The Association's advantages include comprehensive national conferences, networking opportunities, continuing education, and other features. Of special interest to students, recent graduates, and other job seekers is the information ASPA provides about job opportunities. The association maintains a master list of job openings around the country and makes this available on-line through the organization's World Wide Web site.

A recent compilation of job listings included the following:

EMPLOYER	POSITION
U.S. General Accounting Office	Social science analyst
Broward County, Florida	Assistant county administrator
National Cancer Institute	Assistant director for financial management
Kent County, Michigan	Management intern
Clark County, Nevada	Human management intern
Federation for Community Planning	Senior budget analyst
City of Detroit	Director, planning and development department
Soros Foundation	Senior program officer for economic development

More information about the association is available from

American Society for Public Administration
1120 G Street NW, Suite 700
Washington, DC 20005

For Canadians a good source of job ads that include public service positions is

Canadian Employment Weekly
15 Madison Avenue
Toronto, Ontario
Canada M5R 2S2

Each weekly issue of this publication lists more than 500 new position openings including jobs in every province and territory of Canada.

The U.S. government's Office of Personnel Management lists job openings on a continuous basis. This includes posting such openings on its Internet website (to access, simply key in "office of personnel management" while using any on-line search engine). In any given week hundreds of job openings with the federal government are listed. A recent listing included openings for Civil Rights Analyst, Intelligence Support Analyst, Social Science Analyst, Policy Analyst, and a variety of other jobs of potential interest to political science graduates.

A good source of job information at the state legislative level is the National Conference of State Legislatures. This organization, which serves legislators and legislative staff members from across the United States, lists job openings on its website. It also provides a wealth of information about legislative affairs which might be of interest to those considering employment in this area.

For more information, contact

National Conference of State Legislatures
1560 Broadway, Suite 700
Denver, CO 80202

Sample Job Openings in State Legislatures

A recent list of job openings in state legislatures included the following:

Director, Wisconsin Integrated Legislative Information System Staff

Economist, Arizona Joint Legislative Budget Committee

Executive director, Tennessee General Assembly

Executive director, Texas Legislative Reference Library

Fiscal and policy analyst, California Legislative Analyst's Office

Legislative information technology analyst and advisor, North Dakota
    Legislative Council

Policy analyst, Florida Office of Program Policy Analysis and Government
    Accountability

Staff coordinator, Washington State Senate Commerce and Labor
    Committee

Another source of information about government jobs is "Jobs in Government." This is a free on-line service that identifies government job openings. For information, write to

Jobs in Government
P.O. Box 1436
Agoura Hills, CA 91376

Political Parties

Want to get involved in the heart of the political process? If so, one way to go is to seek employment with a major political party. In some cases, you may need to start out as a volunteer first. Here are details for the Democratic and Republican parties.

Democratic National Committee (DNC)
430 S. Capitol Street SE
Washington, DC 20003

Campaign areas for possible work for the DNC as a volunteer or staff member include:

Presidential	State legislative
U.S. Senate	Mayoral
U.S. House	Other state and local races
State gubernatorial	

Republican National Committee (RNC)
310 First Street SE
Washington, DC 20003

Some of the job titles of those who work for the RNC are these:

Chairman	Press secretary
Co-chairman	Political director
Treasurer	Finance director
Chief counsel	Member relations director
Executive director	Administration director
Communications director	

To find out about volunteer or job possibilities, contact the national headquarters of the party in which you are interested. The national offices can also provide you with addresses and phone numbers of state offices for each respective political party.

BECOME MORE KNOWLEDGEABLE ABOUT PUBLIC ISSUES

Your studies to date will have exposed you to an assortment of public policy issues. In preparing to seek positions in government or related areas, it will help your case to demonstrate familiarity with a broad range of issues. Some of the public policy issues with which you may want to demonstrate familiarity include the following:

Affirmative action and equal opportunity	Capital punishment

Censorship in electronic communications

Drug use and related laws and policies

Economic policy

Education reform

Federal versus local government responsibilities

Government-sponsored health care

International trade policy

Political campaign finance

Tax reform

Welfare issues

Reading is one way to maintain a working knowledge of current affairs and topics related to politics and government. News magazines, newspapers, specialized magazines, and books all represent good sources of such information.

Other sources of valuable information include professional associations, both at the national and regional level. For example, the Midwest Political Science Association (MPSA) has 2,500 members. It publishes the *American Journal of Political Science*, which has a subscription base of 4,000.

Every April the MPSA holds a three-day convention in Chicago, attended by more than 2,100 political scientists, students, and practitioners. More than 300 panels are conducted on all areas of political science. Political science students can use such forums not only as an excellent way to gain new knowledge, but also to make contacts and network with others in the field. Other organizations can be similarly helpful. See the list of such groups at the end of this chapter.

TRY AN INTERNSHIP

If you want to gain valuable experience while still a student, consider serving as an intern. Internships in government agencies or other organizations can provide valuable opportunities to supplement learning that takes place in the classroom.

When you serve as an intern, you gain an inside look at what it's like to work in a given career field. You also make contacts that can prove valuable in the future for job reference and other purposes. In some cases internships can lead directly to future employment with the agency you serve.

Some students serve as interns while still completing an undergraduate degree. Others seek internships as a part of master's or doctoral programs.

Typical duties for interns include these examples provided by the National Association of Schools of Public Affairs and Administration.

❏ Conducting research and writing for think tanks

❏ Developing management information systems

❏ Coordinating economic and political surveys

❏ Researching and writing grant proposals

❏ Writing news releases and organizing public relations events

❏ Researching and designing project methodology

❏ Assisting in the implementation of development projects

❏ Conducting evaluations of ongoing projects

STRATEGY FOR FINDING JOBS

In its brochure "Political Science: The Ideal Liberal Arts Major," the American Political Science Association recommends a number of steps for undergraduate majors who will be seeking immediate employment. Among them are the following:

1. Consult professors and college placement counselors to obtain advice about job opportunities and especially about how your own skills and achievements can best be used.

2. Contact government agencies, corporations, newspapers, and professional associations to explore other job opportunities.

3. Prepare a resume that highlights broad analytical and communication skills, internship and job experiences, and knowledge you've gained from political science courses.

4. Send your resume to employers in which you're interested, and consult your placement office to schedule interviews with employers who will be visiting your campus.

5. Talk with people working in organizations that interest you and seek suggestions regarding possible employment.

6. Pursue an internship while still in college with an organization you find interesting.

Remember, it's never too early to begin taking concrete steps that will support your job search. Keep in close touch with professors, counselors, and placement office staff, and maintain records that will help you in seeking employment.

RELATED OCCUPATIONS

The skills that political science majors bring to jobs in government and public service are also valued in a number of related occupations. Here is a small sample of job areas that draw on similar skills to some degree.

Association executive

Corporate manager

Editorial writer

Educational administrator

Government relations specialist for trade union

Health agency manager

Lobbyist

Political pollster

Speechwriter

Volunteer coordinator

PROFESSIONAL ASSOCIATIONS FOR PUBLIC SERVICE PROFESSIONALS

Academy of Political Science
475 Riverside Drive, Suite 1274
New York, NY 10015
Members/Purpose: Serves scholars and others interested in public policy.
Training: Offers issue-related conferences.
Journal/Publication: *Political Science Quarterly*; also publishes books on public policy issues.

American Federation of Government Employees
80 F Street
Washington, DC 20001
Members/Purpose: Serves employees of the federal government in a variety of jobs; 250,000 members.
Training: Holds national meetings.
Journal/Publication: *Government Standard.*

American Federation of State, County and Municipal Employees
1625 L Street NW
Washington, DC 20036

Members/Purpose: Membership includes more than one million government employees. Serves as a union affiliated with the AFL-CIO. Deals with workplace issues of concern to government employees.
Training: Holds biennial meetings.
Journal/Publication: *AFSCME Leader*.

American Political Science Association
1527 New Hampshire Avenue NW
Washington, DC 20036
Members/Purpose: Members include more than 12,000 practitioners, teachers, and students.
Training: Offers conferences and educational materials.
Journal/Publication: *American Political Science Review*; *PS: Political Science and Politics*; variety of other publications.
Jobs: Lists job openings in its *Personnel Newsletter*; offers a job placement service.

Canadian Political Science Association
1 Stewart Street
Ottawa, Ontario
Canada K1N 6H7
Members/Purpose: Members include 1,250 faculty from Canadian colleges and universities, plus politicians and public servants. Supports understanding of the field of political science.
Training: Conference every year.
Journal/Publication: *Canadian Journal of Political Science*; *CPSA Bulletin*; *Canadian Public Policy*; *Careers for Political Scientists*.
Jobs: Lists job openings in its bulletin and on-line.

Inter-University Consortium for Political and Social Research
P.O. Box 1248
Ann Arbor, MI 48106
Members/Purpose: Supports research in the social sciences, including political science.
Training: Conference every other year.
Journal/Publication: *Guide to Resources and Services*.

National Association of Schools of Pubic Affairs and Administration
1120 G Street NW
Washington, DC 20005
Members/Purpose: More than 220 university programs in public affairs and administration and more than 35 associate members. Accredits master's degree programs in public affairs and administration. Promotes excellence in public service education.

Training: Annual conference.
Journal/Publication: *Public Enterprise* newsletter; *NASPAA Faculty Directory*; special papers, reports, and monographs.

National Conference of State Legislatures
1560 Broadway, Suite 700
Denver, CO 80202
Members/Purpose: Serves legislators and legislative staff members from the fifty states. Provides research, publications, consulting services, and educational opportunities.
Training: Sponsors annual meeting; also holds more than twenty seminars and conferences yearly.
Journal/Publication: *State Legislatures* magazine; *Conference Report*; also offers an on-line directory of state legislatures.
Jobs: Lists job openings around the country on its website.

Southern Political Science Association
Department of Political Science
University of North Carolina
Chapel Hill, NC 27599
Members/Purpose: Serves faculty, students, and others interested in the field.
Training: Sponsors conferences.

CHAPTER 11

PATH 2: TEACHING

*I*n studying political science, you have developed an understanding of the basic processes of government and the various aspects of politics. But just how did you acquire this knowledge? In large part it was due to the work of teachers. From your first course in government as a middle or high school student to the varied courses you have taken as a college political science major, teachers have played a key role in your intellectual development.

As you plan ahead, one option is for you to take on the instructional role. After all, a continuing demand exists for people with the right credentials and the appropriate talents to teach political science or related subjects.

Teachers teach. That sounds simple, but in reality they do much more than deliver lectures. Here are just some of the responsibilities of teachers and professors:

- Using various teaching methods to instruct students

- Using audiovisual aids to supplement presentations

- Preparing course objectives and outlines

- Assigning readings, papers, and other student work

- Creating and administering tests

- Evaluating student work and assigning grades

- Advising students

- Participating in committees and professional assignments

- ❏ Performing public or community service
- ❏ Reviewing potential textbooks and instructional support materials
- ❏ Revising and updating curricula
- ❏ Participating in professional development functions
- ❏ Maintaining course and student records
- ❏ Reading and keeping current

For those who teach political science at the college level or government at the middle or high school level, responsibilities are intertwined with the continued study of current events. Political science is an active, ever-changing discipline, and a challenging area to teach.

Certainly, teaching is not for everyone. But if you are a good communicator and feel you might have the potential to share your knowledge with others in an effective manner, this is a career path worth considering.

DEFINITION OF THE CAREER PATH

Political science is a respected academic discipline. It is taught widely in colleges and universities. Students include both those who choose to major or minor in the field and others who take political science classes as a part of their general studies requirements or as electives.

At the high school and middle school level, classes in civics, American government, and related areas are frequently required. Many states and school districts consider it vital that every student take at least one course in this area to promote better citizenship.

The importance of the field has meant there is a continuing demand for men and women qualified to teach it. As a result, a promising career path for those with the right inclinations is teaching political science or related subjects.

Some job titles in this career path follow.

POSSIBLE JOB TITLES

Teacher, middle school (civics)

Teacher, middle school (social science)

Teacher, high school (civics)

Teacher, high school (American government)

Teacher, high school (social science)

Adjunct faculty member (college)

Graduate teaching assistant (college)

Lecturer (college)

Instructor of political science (college)

Assistant professor of political science (college)

Assistant professor of public administration (college)

Associate professor of political science (college)

Associate professor of urban studies (college)

Professor of political science (college)

POSSIBLE EMPLOYERS

If you want to teach political science or related subjects, you can take any of several directions. One approach is to become a professor at a four-year college or university. An alternative is to join the faculty of a community, junior, or technical college. Still another direction is to become a teacher at the middle school or high school level.

Four-Year Colleges and Universities

Teaching at the university or four-year college level is a primary goal of many students who major in political science. Almost every college and university offers courses in political science. This means that a continuing demand exists for faculty with the appropriate training and credentials to teach political science courses.

Well over 2,000 four-year colleges and universities operate in the United States and Canada today. Although not all have undergraduate majors in political science, the majority do, and some also offer master's or doctoral level programs.

At the university level most political science faculty function in two different ways. First, they teach general courses such as Introduction to Political Science. Second, they teach and conduct research in a specialized area in which they hold interest. Here are some of them as identified by the American Association of Political Science:

African-American politics	Methodology
American government and politics	Political communication
Comparative politics	Political parties and interest groups
Country/area politics (Latin American politics, European politics, etc.)	Political philosophy
	Political psychology and socialization
Electoral behavior and public opinion	Politics and history
	Presidential and executive politics
International organizations and law	Public administration
International relations and world politics	Public law and judicial politics
	Public policy
International security and arms control	Urban and ethnic politics
	Women and politics
Legislative politics	

In recent years, the college teaching profession has taken a lot of criticism. Critics contend that professors are under-worked and that they enjoy too many privileges compared to other workers in our society.

While this may be true of some under-motivated faculty, teaching at the college level is actually quite demanding. Professors must not only give lectures and perform other teaching duties, but they are also expected to conduct research, write articles and books, and perform public service, among other duties. They also advise students, serve on committees, develop and refine courses, and spend a great deal of time simply keeping up in their fields.

Even though this life can be challenging, it is also considered by many as one of the most desirable careers available. College faculty enjoy shorter work years, interesting work environments, and hours that usually vary from the nine-to-five routines of much of the business world. At most schools faculty can also qualify for tenure, which provides an unsurpassed measure of job security. All in all, teaching political science in a university or four-year college can be a great career path.

Two-Year Colleges

Even though they may not offer majors in the subject, most community, junior, and technical colleges also offer courses in political science. Students who plan to transfer to four-year schools can take them as part of their associate degree program, and other students also may take a political science course or two to meet general studies requirements or as electives. The result is a demand for faculty to teach political science courses in the two-year college setting.

Sometimes community college faculty specialize in political science and teach only in that discipline. In other instances, especially in smaller schools, faculty teach a second discipline such as history or some other field in the social sciences. Generally this means having completed sufficient courses at the graduate level in both disciplines to meet accrediting agency requirements.

In any case, teaching in two-year colleges is a viable career option for political science majors who are willing to earn a master's degree.

The biggest difference in community college teaching and other college instruction is the course load. In universities faculty may teach as few as two or three courses per semester. In two-year colleges it's more typical to teach five courses per semester. This means community college faculty spend more time in class than their university counterparts. They also tend to devote correspondingly more time in grading papers, preparing lectures, and other instructional tasks. Faculty in two-year schools also tend to spend significant amounts of time advising students, serving on college committees, and performing other duties. They do all this without the help of graduate students or teaching assistants.

All this activity leaves little time for research or writing. But unlike four-year college or university faculty, those teaching in two-year colleges are not generally expected to make this a routine part of their jobs. Instead, they are viewed as professional teachers rather than researchers.

Employers of College Teachers: The Numbers

According to the U.S. Department of Education, there are more than 3,700 colleges and universities operating in the United States today. This means that even in competitive situations, teaching jobs exist on a large scale.

Number of four-year colleges and universities:	2,244
Number of two-year institutions:	1,462
Total:	3,706

FINDING COLLEGE TEACHING JOBS

Finding a teaching job requires an aggressive approach. This is especially true at the college level. Although jobs can be found, chances are that for any given opening, a significant number of candidates will apply. This means that to be successful, you must take advantage of the various sources of information about job openings.

Professional Organizations

Professional organizations provide a great avenue for locating job openings and also for the networking that can help lead to success in obtaining a position.

For example, the American Political Science Association is a solid source of job information. In fact, it maintains a listing of all job openings at the assistant professor and associate professor level in the United States. To access this information, check out the organization's website or write to the address provided at the end of this chapter.

The Canadian Political Science Association (CPSA) provides similar assistance. Job notices are posted in its *Bulletin*, and conferences and meetings provide opportunities for networking. See the list at the end of the chapter for the CPSA address.

Other organizations, both at the national and regional level, can be helpful in the job search process.

Publications

Various publications list job openings in teaching and related areas. Taking the time to peruse such publications can pay off handsomely, at least in terms of finding out about available jobs.

The Chronicle of Higher Education. For teaching opportunities at the college level, a first-rate source of information is the *Chronicle of Higher Education*. This publication includes extensive job listings in every issue. In fact, a typical issue might include hundreds of job openings in colleges throughout the United States and a number in other countries, including several in political science.

Following is a summary of the political science teaching positions appearing in a single issue of the *Chronicle*:

- A tenure-track position at Georgia Southwestern State University in Americus, Georgia

- A position as full professor in the School of Government at the University of Tasmania in Australia

- An assistant professor's position at Wheeling Jesuit University in Wheeling, West Virginia

❑ An assistant professor's position at Troy State University in Troy, Alabama

❑ A tenure track teaching position at Utah Valley State College in Orem, Utah

❑ A post-doctoral position in Political Science and Public Policy at the Woodrow Wilson School of Public and International Affairs at Princeton University in Princeton, New Jersey

Here are sample ads from the *Chronicle* for college teaching jobs.

Political Science: Assistant Professor, tenure-track. Primary teaching responsibilities in comparative politics, international relations and foreign policy. Successful candidate should also have a strong background in political philosophy and American Government. Ph.D. and college teaching preferred, but not necessary. Position begins mid-August 1997. Send letter of application, vita, three letters of recommendation and transcripts to: Political Science Search Committee, Department of Political Science, Ashland University. Review of applications begins March 27 and continues until position is filled. Additional AU information is available at: http://www.ashland.edu. AA/EOE.

Political Science: Southeastern Louisiana University is seeking applicants for a tenure-track Assistant Professor of Political Science available Aug. 17, 1998. Qualifications: Ph.D. required. Areas of concentration are Public Administration, Public Policy, and American Political Institutions. Duties: Teaches the survey courses in Government and Research methods, and will develop and coordinate an internship in government. Provides service activities that benefit the department, college, university. Salary: Commensurate with experience and education. Send resume, three current letters of reference, and a copy of all transcripts (originals required upon employment) to: Political Science Search Committee, SLU. SLU is an AA/ADA/EEO employer.

In addition to job listings, the *Chronicle* publishes a wide variety of information about higher education including book reviews, editorials, and indepth stories about current issues in education, research trends, education financing, professional issues, and other matters. For those who work in higher education or who aspire to employment in academe, it provides fascinating reading and helpful background.

The *Chronicle of Higher Education* is published on a weekly basis except for the third week in August and the last two weeks of December. It is available in college and university libraries and some public libraries, and through subscription at the following address

The Chronicle of Higher Education
1255 Twenty-Third Street NW
Washington, DC 20037

Community College Week. This publication caters specifically to employees at two-year colleges. It includes a section of classified ads for positions at various institutions. Although job listings are not as extensive as those in the *Chronicle of Higher Education*, they are valuable for those interested in pursuing teaching jobs in community, junior, or technical colleges.

To obtain a copy or subscribe, write to

Community College Week
10520 Warwick Avenue, Suite B-8
Fairfax, VA 22030-3136

Professional Contacts

Graduate school professors and university placement offices can also be helpful in the job search process. Their assistance can be useful in obtaining letters of recommendation, locating part-time or temporary teaching positions, and networking with potential employers.

SALARIES EARNED BY POLITICAL SCIENCE PROFESSORS

In 1996–97 political science professors in colleges and universities earned average salaries as outlined below, according to the College and University Personnel Association. For each subsequent year an increase of three to five percent would be a reasonable estimate.

	PUBLIC	PRIVATE
Average of all ranks	$50,748	$50,818
Instructor	$31,479	$31,163
Assistant professor	$38,483	$37,786
Associate professor	$47,288	$46,221
Professor	$62,901	$64,105

Keep in mind that faculty salaries vary according to factors such as these:

Credentials

Faculty rank

Geographical area

Longevity

Type/level of institution

TRAINING AND QUALIFICATIONS

A bachelor's degree is just the starting point for a career in higher education. At the minimum, a master's degree is necessary, and many positions require a doctorate. Completing teacher education courses is not necessary. Instead, the minimum requirement is a master's degree earned in political science or a master's degree in another field with a significant number of graduate courses in political science. Exact requirements for minimum credentials vary with the type of institution and the demands of regional agencies that accredit colleges and universities. The Southern Association of Colleges and Schools, for example, stipulates that all faculty teaching college-level political science courses hold, as a minimum, a master's degree with at least eighteen graduate hours in political science. Many community college faculty hold teaching positions with this level of preparation, although some also hold doctorates.

In most four-year colleges and universities, it is generally expected that faculty hold a doctoral degree. Even if not an absolute requirement, this becomes a matter of practicality in the job search process (if 40 candidates apply for a position and 35 have doctorates, the chances of landing that job with only a master's degree are understandably limited).

If you want to earn a doctorate, you will need dedication and persistence. It takes several years of full-time study beyond the bachelor's degree to earn a doctoral degree (there is no specific time frame; duration varies). Earning a doctorate means more than just taking additional classes of the same type you have completed as an undergraduate. It also means mastering research methodologies and learning to function as an independent researcher.

An excellent brochure is available to guide you on this subject. *Earning a Ph.D. in Political Science* is free on request from

American Political Science Association
1527 New Hampshire Avenue NW
Washington, DC 20036

The Grad School Game

If you're thinking about going on to graduate school and studying political science, here are some strategies to get you there.

Earn Good Grades. Obviously, the higher your grades, the better. If you're still in school but your grades could be better, it's not too late. Most graduate schools will look more closely at the last two years of college and at your major area. If you're already out of school, consider taking a few additional political courses at the bachelor's level and strive for the best possible grades, or do the same thing as a part-time or provisional student at the master's level.

Take the Graduate Record Examination (GRE). This is a fairly standard requirement for graduate school admission. The American Political Science Association recommends that if your score is not in the 80th or 90th percentile, you should consider retaking the exam. In this case putting in some advance studying or investing in a test preparation class can be worthwhile. Also, keep in mind that good grades or other factors can sometimes help offset mediocre scores.

Line Up Good Sources for Letters of Recommendation. Professors who know your work will usually be glad to write recommendation letters. Be sure to contact faculty with sufficient lead time to avoid potential problems in meeting deadlines. Also offer to provide background information that will make writing a letter easier, such as a list of political science courses you have taken or the exact dates and names of courses taken under the professor from whom a letter is requested.

Check Around. Don't just set your sights on one school, but take some time to check out others. According to the American Political Science Association, some 131 colleges and universities in the United States offer doctoral degrees in political science. Others offer master's level programs. With so many different schools from which to choose, the odds are on your side of finding at least one school that matches your particular interests and abilities.

OPPORTUNITIES FOR MINORITIES

If you are a minority student, you should be aware of some special opportunities available to you. Many universities offer scholarship and fellowship programs that provide support for graduate study as well as special programs to promote diversity.

The American Political Science Association offers these three programs designed to identify and provide assistance to minorities:

- ❑ The *Minority Fellowship Program* is a fellowship designed to increase the number of minority Ph.D.s in political science. It also encourages colleges and universities to provide financial assistance to minority students.

- ❑ The *Ralph Bunche Summer Institute* is a three-week program offered every year that introduces African-American students to the world of graduate study and encourages them to pursue doctoral degrees.

- ❑ The *Minority Identification Project* fosters cooperation among graduate schools and bachelor's-level programs in political science to develop the profession by encouraging talented students to undertake graduate studies.

For details about any of these three programs, contact

American Political Association
1527 New Hampshire Avenue NW
Washington, DC 20036

TEACHING HIGH SCHOOL

Almost every high school offers courses in civics, government, or related areas. This represents an area of real job potential for those willing to obtain the right credentials and who can function effectively in teaching children.

To prepare for teaching at the high school level, a political science major must be combined with courses designed to prepare students to become certified as teachers. Details of this process vary in different states and among different colleges and universities. Generally, this involves completing courses in teacher education, successfully completing a student teaching experience, and passing standardized examinations.

The most common standard for teaching at the high school level is a bachelor's degree plus certification or licensure to teach. The latter is usually obtained by taking education courses and passing a comprehensive examination required by the state board of education or equivalent body in the state where you live or plan to teach.

At one time preparing to teach meant majoring in Education (sometimes called Teacher Education) while also taking courses in subjects you planned to teach. Nowadays, many colleges and universities follow a different model.

Here, you major in a specific discipline in which you are interested and also take a selection of education courses, including student teaching.

If you are a political science major, you can qualify to teach at the high school level by completing all the requirements for a degree in political science, plus completing the education courses required by your college and state. Ideally, this is done concurrently with your other studies. If you are near the end of your bachelor's degree or have already completed it and then decide to pursue a secondary teaching career, you will need to go back and complete these education requirements.

An alternative to this approach offered by some colleges is to complete a special program that brings you in compliance with the necessary requirements. For example, Keene State College in New Hampshire offers a "Post-Baccalaureate Teacher Certification Program." This program allows liberal arts graduates to become certified teachers. Another approach is to earn a master's degree in education, completing teacher certification requirements in the process.

Typical course requirements for licensure to teach (course titles vary by institution) are as follows:

The School and the Student	Evaluation of Learning
Introduction to Educational Media	Secondary Curriculum and Instructional Techniques
Accommodations for Exceptional Learners	Education in the United States
Management of Instruction	Student Teaching

HIGH SCHOOL TEACHING—MORE THAN JUST TEACHING

Teaching in high school can be very different from teaching at the college level. In addition to time spent on in-class teaching, grading papers, and performing related instructional work, working as a high school government or civics teacher can mean performing tasks such as the following:

- Serving as an advisor to a student club or organization
- Performing hall or bus duty
- Eating lunch with students and supervising their behavior
- Disciplining unruly students
- Driving students to extracurricular activities (such as a model United Nations session)

- Chaperoning at a dance
- Meeting with parents on a routine basis
- Meeting with parents when a student is experiencing or creating special problems
- Serving on an accreditation self-study team
- Serving on a committee to hire a new teacher or administrator
- Ordering textbooks, software, or supplies
- Coordinating mock elections

Following is a listing of skills high school teachers need for success (adapted from requirements at Radford University).

Typical Skills Expected of High School Teachers

- Planning, implementing, and evaluating instruction
- Managing classroom and administrative tasks
- Collecting and interpreting student data
- Promoting students' cognitive, psychomotor, and socioaffective development
- Providing for individual and cultural differences
- Applying knowledge of social forces that affect professional responsibility in a global society
- Working with others in conducting professional tasks and in pursuing professional development
- Applying a breadth and depth of knowledge of the teaching specialty area

TEACHER SALARIES

Do teachers make good salaries? That depends on who you ask. Many teachers complain about unattractive salaries, and they have a point. Compared to earnings of many other professionals, teacher pay is low. But at the same time, salaries are not really that bad. In an era when many college graduates find it difficult to find jobs following graduation, a job in teaching offers solid if unspectacular pay as well as good benefits such as health insurance and retirement plans.

In addition, teachers enjoy more time off than almost any other workers. Most work under nine- or ten-month contracts, providing for significant time off in the summer as well as during holidays. Many teachers use this time to pursue part-time jobs, run their own businesses, or otherwise supplement their income. They may also take advantage of this time to attend graduate school, travel, or pursue other personal interests.

Salary levels for teachers are usually determined at the local level. Most school districts follow a strict salary schedule based on education and years spent on the job.

Teachers in Virginia, for example, earned the following minimum salaries in 1997–98, with actual salaries varying from one school division to the next and with individual salary increases received in previous years. Other states offer comparable salaries, although actual figures vary.

Minimum Salary, Bachelor's Degree: $25,272
Minimum Salary, Bachelor's plus 5 years experience: $27,157
Minimum Salary, Master's Degree: $27,157

With additional years of experience, salaries move up into the 30s and 40s, and some senior teachers earn more than $50,000 annually.

Comparable salaries are earned by teachers in other states, with higher salaries the norm in major cities and areas where living costs are higher.

For teachers in private high schools, salaries tend to be somewhat lower than those paid public school teachers although actual salaries vary from one school to the next.

FINDING HIGH SCHOOL AND MIDDLE SCHOOL TEACHING JOBS

Seeking a teaching position in a middle school or high school usually involves more of a local emphasis than does the college hiring process. While most colleges advertise regionally or nationally for full-time vacancies, the typical school district relies more on local or statewide advertising. Thus a good way to learn about openings is to consult the want ad sections of newspapers.

An increasingly productive way to seek out teaching jobs is to use the Internet. Many school districts now post information about their schools, and sometimes about job openings, on the Internet.

An outstanding example is EDNET, a free on-line service that lists teaching openings. From its base in Woodland Hills, California, this service posts the following:

❑ Job openings in Southern California schools

❑ Selected openings in other parts of California and in other states

❑ A list of California's school districts

Other similar services may be available for your area or for states or regions in which you're interested. To locate them, just use any Internet search engine and seek out "teaching jobs" or similar identifiers.

Another strategy is to contact school districts directly. Ask for a list of any anticipated job openings, and submit a resume or application.

Some prospective teachers use substitute teaching as a way to get started. Often, those who have served as substitutes become a "known quantity" and may gain an edge when full-time positions become available.

EDUCATIONAL ADMINISTRATION

A career focus closely related to teaching is educational administration. Every school and college has administrators who manage its academic affairs as well as other areas ranging from executive management to administrative support.

Typically, administrative personnel in the educational setting start out as teachers and then progress to administrative roles. In the middle school or high school setting, a teacher interested in administrative work might take on a role such as assistant principal. This might require completion of additional classes or a degree in educational administration, coupled with sufficient teaching experience. After spending some time as an assistant principal, an administrator might move on to a principal's position, and from there to a central office position such as curriculum coordinator, director of pupil services, or assistant superintendent of schools. A relatively few administrators might eventually assume top-level roles such as superintendent of schools or state-level positions such as state superintendent of schools.

At the college level a professor of political science might take on the role of department chairperson. In higher education no specific training in administration is necessarily required. Quite often faculty learn "on the job" once they are appointed to administrative positions, although some faculty who aspire to administrative jobs complete master's or doctoral degrees in administrative or management fields. Some faculty accept administrative roles only temporarily and then return to teaching. Others become career administrators. They may go on to hold positions such as dean, vice president, or college president.

Following are some typical job titles for educational administrators.

Job Titles in Educational Administration

Public School Administrative Positions

Assistant principal

Principal

Director of curriculum

Director of instruction

Assistant superintendent of schools

Superintendent of schools

Associate superintendent of schools

Director of finance and administration

Director of transportation

College and University Administrative Positions

Department chairperson

Division chairperson

Dean, College of Arts and Sciences

Associate vice president

Vice president for academic affairs

Vice president for advancement

Vice president for administration

Provost

President

Director of planning

Assistant to the president

Director of enrollment management

Registrar

Director of institutional advancement

Director of institutional research

Dean of instruction

Dean of student services

RELATED CAREERS

In addition to educational administration, political science can also lead to other career paths related to teaching. The skills used in the classroom are not unlike those used in a number of other occupations. Consider the following job titles as a beginning list. Then investigate these and other positions that draw on the skill base you have developed.

Corporate trainer

Educational consultant

Human resources professional

Policy analyst

Public affairs specialist

Researcher

Sales representative, educational publishing company

Textbook editor

Textbook writer

Tutor

PROFESSIONAL ASSOCIATIONS FOR TEACHERS, PROFESSORS, AND RELATED PROFESSIONALS

Association of Social and Behavioral Scientists (ASBS)
American University, Department of History
4400 Massachusetts Avenue NW
Washington, DC 20016
Members/Purpose: Provides a professional network for social and behavioral scientist and related professionals.
Training: Annual meeting.

American Association of University Professors
1012 Fourteenth Street NW, Suite 500
Washington, DC 20005
Members/Purpose: Serves college and university faculty.
Training: Meetings and other conferences.
Journal/Publication: *Academe*; also publishes annual faculty salary report.

National Association of Professional Educators
412 1st Street NE
Washington, DC 20000
Members/Purpose: Serves as an alternative to teacher unions. Membership includes 75,000 professional educators.
Training: Annual meeting.
Journal/Publication: *Professional Education Newsletter*.

National Council for the Social Studies
3501 Newark Street NW
Washington, DC 20016
Members/Purpose: Members include 22,000 teachers of social studies including teachers of civics, political science, and other fields.

Training: Annual conference.
Journal/Publication: *Arts and Humanities in Social Sciences*; *Cooperative Learning in the Social Studies Classroom*; *The Social Studies Professional.*

National Education Association
1201 16th Street NW
Washington, DC 20036
Members/Purpose: Professional organization advancing the cause of public education. More than 2.2 million members represent all areas of education from preschool to graduate programs.
Training: Meetings and conferences.
Journal/Publication: *NEA Today*; *NEA Focus.*

Social Science Research Council
605 3rd Avenue
New York, NY 10158
Members/Purpose: Members are social scientists in a variety of fields, including political scientists and faculty. Promotes interdisciplinary research.
Journal/Publication: *Social Science Research Council Items.*

CHAPTER TWELVE

PATH 3: LAW

*E*veryone has heard lawyer jokes. But in reality the law remains one of the most attractive professions in our society. Men and women who work as attorneys enjoy interesting work, excellent incomes, and a high level of prestige.

Students who want to become lawyers need not major in any one discipline while studying as undergraduates. In fact, "prelaw" majors can study in virtually any liberal arts field, and some outside the traditional arts and sciences, and still go on to law school. It is in law school that prospective attorneys acquire the specific knowledge and skills they will need to become practicing lawyers.

At the same time many students who aspire to become lawyers major in political science. There is a natural connection between the study of political science and the study of law. Since political science covers government and politics, and attorneys deal with the interpretation of laws promulgated by government, those who study and understand political science may put themselves in a favorable position for understanding our legal system and the ways attorneys work within it.

DEFINITION OF THE CAREER PATH

Sometimes they're called lawyers. Other times they're labeled attorneys. In either case, these professionals act as advocates and advisors. They represent opposing parties in court and advise clients about legal matters. In the process, lawyers interpret the law and apply it to business and personal affairs affecting their clients.

A major part of an attorney's job is conducting research. This involves studying laws and judicial decisions that might apply to the particular circumstances of a given case. In the past this meant consulting law books, journals, and other written records. While that is still a part of the job, using computers to conduct research is an increasingly important part of a lawyer's work.

Lawyers also spend a great deal of their time communicating. They write and edit documents, present oral information, and interview clients and witnesses.

While the general title for this occupation is *lawyer* or *attorney*, titles may also be more specific. Here are just some job titles for lawyers.

POSSIBLE JOB TITLES

Admiralty lawyer	Probate lawyer
Corporation lawyer	Prosecuting attorney
Criminal lawyer	Real estate lawyer
Insurance attorney	Tax attorney
Patent lawyer	Title attorney

Some lawyers, especially those operating their own practices or working in small firms, practice in a variety of areas. But many lawyers specialize. Law is a complex subject requiring a great deal of in-depth knowledge not only to begin practicing in the first place, but to maintain ongoing competency. For this reason, and for business purposes such as attracting specific types of clients, it is often more practical to focus on one or two areas.

Some specialty areas include the following:

Advocacy	International law
Constitutional law	Juvenile law
Copyright and patent law	Labor law
Corporate and commercial law	Race and the law
Criminal law	Tax law
Education law	Wills and trusts
Environmental law	

POSSIBLE EMPLOYERS

Some attorneys are self-employed, operating their own law practices. Others work for law firms, government agencies, corporations, or other organizations. Some possible employers of lawyers are listed below.

Banks	Professional associations
City governments	Real estate agencies
Colleges	Religious organizations
County governments	State agencies
Insurance companies	U.S. Department of Defense
Interest groups	U.S. Department of Justice
Manufacturing firms	U.S. Treasury Department
Private law firms	

TRAINING AND QUALIFICATIONS

Becoming a lawyer is possible only after intense training. This normally includes a combination of college, law school, and the passing of a bar exam. Requirements vary in different states. In California, for example, students may study law by correspondence and then take the bar exam.

Most students who pursue law first earn a bachelor's degree and then complete three years of law school. Then they take the bar exam required in their state, and also complete an ethics examination.

APPLYING TO LAW SCHOOL

If you're a political science major or recent graduate and decide to shoot for a legal career, the first step is applying for admission to law school.

Most law schools require the following from applicants:

1. A completed application for admission. This is available on request from any law school.

2. An application fee. The amount varies, but $50 is typical. Some schools require an additional deposit from those who are accepted to confirm the acceptance.

3. Letters of recommendation. Usually, these are from professors who know your work.

4. Transcripts of your college credits and grades. Initially, transcript details can be forwarded through the Law School Data Assembly Service (LSDAS), a special clearinghouse that provides this service. After acceptance, official copies of transcripts will be be required.

5. Test scores. Your scores from the Law School Admission Test (LSAT) will be a necessary part of the application package (see following section for more details).

For more information about applying to law school, write to

American Bar Association
750 N. Lake Shore Drive
Chicago, IL 60611

A good source of information about Canadian law schools is

Council of Canadian Law Deans
57 Louis-Pasteur
Ottawa, Ontario
Canada K1N 6N5

The Law School Admission Test

There's almost no getting around it. If you want to go to law school, you'll have to take the Law School Admission Test (LSAT). Most law schools in the United States and Canada require prospective students to take this test.

Sitting for the LSAT is no picnic, but the experience is not all that different from taking the SAT or other standardized tests you took before enrolling in college. The exam is a half-day test consisting of multiple choice questions broken up into five sections taking 35 minutes each, plus a half-hour writing sample.

Scores range from 120 to 180, with the latter being the highest score. The writing sample is not scored but is sent on to the schools where you apply.

To prepare for the LSAT, you might want to purchase a test preparation book or check one out from a library. Or you might consider enrolling in a review course or seminar.

Thinking Skills Measured by the LSAT

❑ Ability to read and comprehend complex texts with accuracy and insight

❑ Ability to organize and manage information and draw reasonable inferences from it

❑ Ability to reason critically

❑ Ability to analyze and evaluate the reasoning and arguments of others

STUDYING LAW

Once you start law school, you will be immersed in a thorough and demanding curriculum. In most cases completing a *Juris Doctor* degree (the typical degree pursued by most law students) requires three years of full-time study. The actual time varies by school, type of degree, and whether you attend part-time, which is an option offered at some law schools.

The courses taken to earn a law degree vary. A typical pattern is to take a fairly rigid schedule of courses the first year, and then to have more flexibility in choosing courses based on personal interests and plans for specializing in specific areas of law.

At the Vanderbilt University School of Law in Nashville, Tennessee, students are required to take the following courses during the first year of study:

Fall Semester

Contracts

Legal Process and Institutions of Lawmaking

Legal Writing and Introduction to Lawyering I

Torts

Spring Semester

Civil Procedure

Constitutional Law

Criminal Law

Legal Writing and Introduction to Lawyering II

Property

Later courses can then be selected from scores of course offerings including the following:

American Legal History

Children and the Law

Constitutional Tort Litigation

Copyright Law

Corporation Finance

Criminal Law

Environmental Law

Federal Tax Law

Health Law and Policy   Trial Advocacy

Immigration Law

Other law schools offer their own course selections and programs. One innovative model can be found at the Case Western University School of Law in Cleveland, Ohio, where interdisciplinary studies are emphasized. Students often take courses offered by other graduate schools within the university. Along with the *Juris Doctor* (JD) degree, they can choose from four joint degree programs as follows:

JD-MBA (master of business   JD-MSSA (social work)
administration)
                                    JD-MNO (nonprofit organizations)
JD-MA (legal history)

In addition students can work with school officials to create their own joint programs. The overall approach is that attorneys need practical as well as theoretical knowledge.

EARNINGS

Lawyers are generally well paid. In fact, the attractive earnings potential for a career in law is one of the main incentives for many people who pursue this field.

Like any complex field, salaries actually vary quite widely. Senior partners in successful law firms or lawyers holding high-level corporate positions may earn several hundred thousand dollars a year, or even more. At the other extreme, a newly hired associate in a small firm may be paid $35,000 annually.

In its annual salary survey published in February 1998, *Working Woman* magazine reported the following average salaries for men and women working in the field of law.

General counsel (corporate)	$365,000
Partner/shareholder (private)	$174,719
U.S. Attorney (public)	$115,700
Corporate attorney	$ 99,000
Associate (private)	$ 75,761
Lawyer (overall)	$ 59,748

In government jobs (such as U.S. attorneys and assistant attorneys) salary ranges follow strict guidelines established by the government. In the private sector salaries have more room for difference. Law firms and corporations may establish their own salary levels based on previous company policy and current market conditions. This may vary quite widely. Obviously, a New York firm with 150 lawyers will have greater resources than a two-person law firm in a small town in Alabama. Also, some attorneys prefer to start their own practices. In this case earnings will depend entirely on the success of the firm, as with any small business.

WORKING CONDITIONS

Lawyers work in courtrooms, right? They sit at tables with their clients or walk around performing for the judge or jury like Perry Mason, Ally McBeal, or other characters from innumerable movies and television shows.

Well, that is true some of the time, for some lawyers. But attorneys spend a great deal of time in settings outside of courtrooms. And some never set foot in court.

The truth is, work settings for attorneys vary widely. Lawyers work in their own offices and those of colleagues, in conference rooms, in law libraries, and in other locations. Generally, such locations are quite comfortable, with all the trappings one would expect of modern offices. For those who are just getting started or who work for nonprofit organizations, though, office settings may be quite modest. They may be small, cramped, and simply appointed. At the other extreme senior partners or attorneys holding high-level corporate positions may enjoy large, luxurious offices.

Outside of law offices and court facilities, lawyers may perform a variety of field work, depending on job assignments and the nature of work in which they specialize. For example, an attorney may spend hours sitting in a dusty, poorly lit basement of a government building, poring through old documents. An attorney preparing for a lawsuit may visit the hospital room of an accident victim and the site where an automobile crash occurred. Another may fly to another city to take a deposition or interview a potential witness.

Perhaps the most important factor in working conditions for attorneys is not location, but time. Many lawyers put in very long hours. This is especially common for attorneys who are just starting their careers. A young lawyer employed by a large law firm may be expected to work sixty hours a week or more. Senior lawyers may also work long hours, although some enjoy a more favorable schedule than beginning attorneys.

For lawyers employed by government agencies or nonprofit organizations, working hours may vary. In some cases a forty-hour work week is the norm.

FINDING JOBS

Law is a highly desirable field. So it's no surprise that it is also a competitive one. Those who want to practice law not only face stiff competition in getting admitted to law school, but they also can encounter difficulty in landing good jobs.

According to the U.S. Department of Education, the number of law school graduates has increased about 8 percent over the last five years. More than 30,000 men and women graduate from American law schools every year. When their numbers are added to the large number of attorneys already practicing law, the job market can be tight.

This doesn't mean those considering law should give up their hopes. But anyone who sets a goal of becoming an attorney should be aware of this situation and be willing to work diligently in the job search process.

A primary method of finding jobs in this field is to use the processes established by universities to help their graduates find jobs. These processes vary from one school to another, but virtually all law schools consider helping graduates find jobs to be one of their responsibilities, and provide services accordingly.

Typically, assistance in helping students includes services such as the following:

❑ Job fairs where prospective employers visit a campus and interview students who will be graduating during that academic year

❑ Help in scheduling on-campus interviews on an individualized basis

❑ Assistance in scheduling off-campus interviews

❑ Correspondence with prospective employers and posting of job openings on bulletin boards, web pages, and other sites

❑ Development of recruitment handbooks that profile prospective graduates

❑ Publication of lists of job openings

❑ Individualized counseling and advisement regarding the career search process

At the Vanderbilt University School of Law, for example, an on-campus recruitment program is held every year during the fall semester. About 350 employers take part, representing 30 states and the District of Columbia. Both second-year and third-year students participate. Students in their first year are also assisted in finding summer employment.

In addition, prospective law school graduates can conduct their own job searches using a variety of resources. This might include singling out prospective employers and sending them introductory letters with resumes, using personal contacts of friends and family, and consulting publications that list job openings for attorneys.

Some companies provide fee-based information about job openings. For example, a Washington, D.C., firm lists hundreds of summer positions for law students in its annual *Summer Legal Employment Guide*. For information, write to

Legal Reports
1010 Vermont Avenue NW
Washington, DC 20005

You may also be able to find publications of this type in college career services offices or law libraries.

RELATED OCCUPATIONS

Persons who hold law degrees don't necessarily practice law. They may go on to take other related positions such as judgeships. Or they may work for corporations, write about law-related matters, or perform other functions.

In addition, a number of other occupations carry related responsibilities. Many related positions do not require law degrees but might be of potential interest to those who have studied political science.

Judges

As a college student, you may have sat in class and thought that someday you'd like to take on the role of professor (if so, be sure to look at options outlined in Path 2). For lawyers, a similar line of thought is to aspire to become a judge.

Some lawyers do move on to hold positions as judges. Although the number of judges is relatively small compared to the number of attorneys, this is a reasonable goal for those who become attorneys and have the right combination of drive and intelligence.

Types of judges include the following:

Administrative law judges	General trial court judges
Appellate court judges	Magistrates
County court judges	Municipal court judges

Other Related Occupations

Appeals board referee	Legal investigator
Arbitrator	Legal writer
Contract clerk	Paralegal
Hearing officer	Patent agent
Law professor	Private investigator
Law school dean	Title examiner
Legal assistant	

KEEPING UP THROUGH READING

To learn more about law, read publications about the subject. Several books and magazines of interest are listed at the end of this book.

An excellent source of information for attorneys working on their own or those working in small firms is *Lawyers Weekly*. This publication includes a national version (*Lawyers Weekly USA*) as well as state-specific versions for Massachusetts, Michigan, Maine, North Carolina, Ohio, Rhode Island, and Virginia. For information, write to

Lawyers Weekly
41 West Street
Boston, MA 02111

PROFESSIONAL ASSOCIATIONS FOR LAWYERS, ATTORNEYS, AND RELATED PROFESSIONALS

American Bar Association
750 N. Lake Shore Drive
Chicago, IL 60611
Members/Purpose: Serves attorneys, law students, and others interested in the legal profession. The organization includes 22 sections and more than 80 commissions.
Training: Sponsors conferences and seminars; provides educational materials.
Journal/Publication: Publishes *ABA Journal* as well as other publications.

Job Listings: Offers job information to students and on-line links to employment sites.

Association of American Law Schools
1201 Connecticut Avenue NW, Suite 800
Washington, DC 20036-2605
Members/Purpose: Works to improve the legal profession through legal education. Serves as the learned society for law teachers.
Training: Annual meeting plus five to six conferences a year.
Journal/Publication: Quarterly newsletter; *Directory of Law Teachers.*

The Attorneys Group
292 Madison Avenue
New York, NY 10017
Members/Purpose: Attorneys and law students; provides support services and economic benefits.
Training: Sponsors workshops.
Journal/Publication: *TAG Brief.*

The Canadian Bar Association
902-50 O'Connor
Ottawa, Ontario
Canada K1P 6L2
Members/Purpose: Serves attorneys and law students.
Training: Sponsors conferences.

Council of Canadian Law Deans
57 Louis-Pasteur
Ottawa, Ontario
Canada K1N 6N5
Members/Purpose: Coordinates activities among Canada's 20 law schools plus an undergraduate law department at Carleton University.
Journal/Publication: Maintains a list of Canadian law schools.

Federal Bar Association
1815 H Street NW
Washington, DC 20006
Members/Purpose: Members include 15,000 attorneys, judges, legislators, and others; supports continuing education and community service.
Training: Holds annual meeting.
Journal/Publication: *Federal Bar News and Journal.*

Law School Admission Council
Law Services
661 Penn Street

Newtown, PA 18940

Members/Purpose: Nonprofit organization whose members are 194 law schools in the United States and Canada. Administers the Law School Admission Test (LSAT).

Journal/Publication: *Financial Aid for Law School: A Preliminary Guide*; *Thinking About Law School: A Minority Guide.*

CHAPTER THIRTEEN

PATH 4: NONPROFIT MANAGEMENT

While the typical political science major might envision a future career in government, law, or teaching, another area of potential employment is often overlooked: working as a manager or other professional in a nonprofit organization. Yet taken together, nonprofit organizations represent a huge area of employment.

At the end of each of the preceding three chapters, you may have noticed a list of professional organizations. These groups can be helpful in a variety of ways. But did it occur to you that they also represent employment potential? Virtually every professional association employs a staff of managers and other employees.

Actually, the term *nonprofit* is somewhat misleading because it is so often connected with volunteerism and in some ways is separated from the "business" world. But in fact, nonprofit activities are big business. Such organizations may not have making money as their main goal, but in other respects they operate very much like businesses. This includes maintaining a staff of paid employees whose job it is to carry out the work of the organization.

For example, the American Society of Association Executives employs a president and an executive vice president to manage its affairs. The organization also employs a full-time staff of more than 130 persons.

The story is similar in other organizations. Some have only a few staff members, while others provide employment for scores of workers. Some have objectives related to the political process, government, or related matters. For them a political science background can be especially helpful. For countless other organizations a college degree in any liberal arts field, including political science, can provide the background for an entry-level position—or with additional job experience, a variety of positions including top-level executive management.

DEFINITION OF THE CAREER PATH

Serving in nonprofit management can take on a variety of forms. Some jobs consist of providing overall administrative duties. A common job title in the nonprofit sector is executive director, with the president being a member of the board that oversees the group rather than an employee. In this structure the executive director is the top-level paid employee. Related positions include titles such as associate executive director and assistant director.

In some organizations a business-type structure is utilized with the top paid position being that of president. Related positions include vice president, associate vice president, and assistant vice president. Often a voluntary board of directors provides oversight, headed by a chairperson.

Other positions commonly include titles such as director and coordinator. Examples include director of member services and public information coordinator. Following are some representative job titles in nonprofit organizations.

POSSIBLE JOB TITLES

Assistant vice president

Associate executive director

Associate vice president

Chief operating officer

Development associate

Development director

Development officer

Direct marketing coordinator

Director of affiliate services

Director of communications

Director of education

Director of finance and administration

Director of public affairs

Executive administrator

Executive director

Field director

Major gift officer

Media relations director

Planned giving specialist

President

Program associate

Program director

Program officer

Public relations coordinator

Regional development manager

Senior consultant

Senior grants administrator

Senior program officer

Senior vice president

Vice president

Vice president for development

Volunteer coordinator

POSSIBLE EMPLOYERS

Where does employment in the nonprofit sector lead? A career in this area might mean working for a private foundation, a professional organization, an interest group, a charity, or any of a number of other organizations.

Foundations

How would you like to have a job where a major duty is giving away money? That's the situation for many managers who work for private foundations. These nonprofit organizations exist to hold and manage funds that have been donated by wealthy individuals, families, corporations, and others. In most cases that also involves giving away funds in the form of grants. In fact, some kinds of foundations are required by law to give away at least 5 percent of their investment assets each year.

Thousands of private and corporate foundations exist in the United States and Canada. Some are small, obscure entities virtually unknown except to a few recipients of their assets and the bank officers or others who manage them. Others, such as the Ford Foundation and the Kellogg Foundation, are huge enterprises holding billions of dollars in assets and employing hundreds of people.

The Philadelphia Foundation is an example of a community foundation, an organization that serves the needs of specific cities or communities. This foundation had over $144 million in assets in 1997, when it distributed nearly $9 million in grants to nonprofit groups in southeastern Pennsylvania. Recipients of grants included neighborhood revitalization groups, human service programs, schools and education projects, health-care initiatives, and other groups.

According to a survey conducted by the Columbus Foundation of Columbus, Ohio, community foundations receive more than $2 billion each year in donations. Over twenty such groups have more than $200 million in assets each, and more than forty hold assets in excess of $100 million. As these foundations continue to grow and others are formed, job opportunities are expanding for those with an interest in nonprofit management.

Another type of foundation is the family foundation, where the members of a family have set up an organization to honor family members and dispense funds, typically to meet local needs or support a special interest area.

A number of companies have established corporate foundations where a portion of profits is used to make donations for purposes consistent with the company's objectives or philosophy. For instance, the McDonald's Foundation supports the needs of children through a variety of grant programs.

Regardless of the type of foundation, all but the smallest or those that are inactive find it necessary to employ paid staff. Typical job titles within foundations include:

Director of development	President
Executive director	Senior program officer
Field officer	Vice president
Grants administrator	Vice president for communications
Grants manager	Vice president for programs

SOME MAJOR FOUNDATIONS

Foundation	Location
Abell Foundation	Baltimore, Maryland
Annenberg Foundation	St. David's, Pennsylvania
Carnegie Corporation	New York, New York
Danforth Foundation	St. Louis, Missouri
Lilly Endowment	Indianapolis, Indiana
Ford Foundation	New York, New York
Heinz Endowments	Pittsburgh, Pennsylvania
W. M. Keck Foundation	Los Angeles, California
W. K. Kellogg Foundation	Troy, Michigan
Robert Wood Foundation	Princeton, New Jersey

John D. and Catherine T.
    MacArthur Foundation   Chicago, Illinois

Pew Charitable Trusts   Philadelphia, Pennsylvania

Rockefeller Foundation   New York, New York

ASSOCIATIONS

A great American tradition is the state, regional, or national association that brings together people with common interests. Often this revolves around occupations. For example, associations listed at the end of the career paths chapters in this book are based on occupational interests.

Examples of associations include the following:

Alabama Textile Manufacturers   Florida Recreation and Park
    Association   Association

Alaska Bar Association   Hawaii Credit Union League

American Business Women's   Home Care Association of New York
    Association   State

American Payroll Association   Oklahoma Municipal League

California Automotive Wholesalers' Self Storage Association
    Association

INTEREST GROUPS

Want to save the whales? Stop child abuse? Promote the use of atomic energy? Eliminate abortion? Expand the availability of abortion? Whatever your interest, chances are at least one special interest group exists to bring together people with common interests and promote their agendas. Like other nonprofit organizations, interest groups typically employ staff to coordinate their affairs. Examples of interest groups include:

Center for Advancement of Public   Children's Defense Fund
    Policy
                                     Committee to Protect Journalists
Center for Law and Social Policy
                                     Dispute Resolution Center
Center for Responsive Politics

Domestic Violence Program

Economic Policy Institute

Environmental Defense Fund

Family Resource Coalition

Fund for Peace

Hispanic Community Talent
Inventory

National Center for Family Literacy

National Center for Strategic
Nonprofit Planning and
Community Leadership

National Rifle Association

Partners in Parenting

Public Employees Roundtable

Sierra Club

Waste Awareness and Reduction
Network

Women's Information Network
Against Breast Cancer

CHARITIES

Many organizations exist specifically to raise funds for needy causes. They are not necessarily a completely separate category from interest groups or other organizations, but the emphasis is usually on collecting funds for redistribution to groups or individuals who need assistance or to fund research or other efforts aimed at helping those in need.

Examples of charities include:

American Heart Association

American Lung Association

Big Brothers/Big Sisters

Family Abuse Services

Habitat for Humanity

Legal Aid Service

Neighborhood Justice Center

Parent Assistance League

Salvation Army

Student Rural Health Coalition

SAMPLE JOB ANNOUNCEMENT

The following job opening was advertised by the Alzheimer's Association. Although this particular opening required several years of job experience, it is typical of the kinds of jobs a political science graduate might qualify for in the nonprofit sector.

OPENING: POLICY ANALYST

The Health for Seniors Association, a national voluntary health agency with a strong grassroots chapter network, seeks an experienced policy analyst/advocate in its Washington, D.C., office to lead and direct its state health and long-term care policy work nationwide. The Analyst manages the Association's award-winning state policy clearinghouse, coordinates strategic policy analysis, and develops collaborations with national organizations of state officials.

Specific job functions include the following:

- Develop Association positions, strategies, model legislation, and supporting materials on priority issues, and promote their effective use by chapter advocates in the states.
- Monitor state policy developments to identify health issues and opportunities for advocacy.
- Facilitate regular exchange of information and strategies on state issues among health advocates in the chapter network.
- Publish a bimonthly State Policy Report on health issues for state advocates and public officials.
- Develop collaborations with national organizations of state officials, including conferences, workshops, and policy reports, to further the Association's state policy objectives.

Successful candidates will have a degree in political science, health policy, or a related field and 3–5 years experience in state legislative or health policy, and proven success in coordinating advocacy efforts.

The position also requires experience in managing computerized databases to maintain a clearinghouse of advocacy issues for the Association's 150 chapters nationwide.

EARNINGS

Salaries paid by nonprofit organizations vary enormously. For a small community agency salaries may lag far behind those of private businesses. For a large national organization salaries may be quite good, especially for upper-level managers.

On average, salaries earned in the nonprofit sector are not as high as those for comparable positions in private business. Certainly, such benefits as stock options and profit sharing plans are not available in the nonprofit world. And since the dominant purpose is performing some type of service, the culture of most nonprofit organizations runs counter to the profit-making mentality of businesses.

Still, salaries can be attractive for managers in nonprofit groups. In addition, fringe benefits can be attractive, and attractive features such as deferred compensation are becoming more common.

The *Nonprofit Times* conducts an annual survey of salaries of subscribers. In its survey published in the February 1998 issue, it found anticipated 1998 salary averages for executives in nonprofit organizations as follows.

Chief executive officer	$65,617
Chief financial officer	$46,176
Program director	$41,699
Planned giving officer	$41,278
Development director	$41,493
Major gifts officer	$45,646
Chief of direct marketing	$38,653
Director of volunteers	$28,882

The *Nonprofit Times* notes that salaries vary widely not only by type of organization, but also by its size. Chief executives in organizations with annual budgets of more than $10 million, for example, earn average salaries of more than $100,000.

Results of a 1997 survey conducted by the American Society of Association Executives (ASAE) found similar results. As reported in *Association Management* magazine, the average salary for an association chief executive officer was more than $116,000. The median salary (that is, the salary for which one-half of salaries fall below and one-half are higher), was nearly $96,000 in 1996.

Averages for other positions as reported by Association Management included the following:

Association/foundation	$69,816
Deputy chief executive	$89,622
Education/certification	$57,751
Government/lobbying	$78,242
Human resources	$64,055
Member services	$48,221
Public relations	$63,302

ASAE surveys have found that a number of factors affect salary levels. Significant factors include size of organization, size of staff, association income, geographical area, and experience on the job.

TRAINING AND QUALIFICATIONS

In many cases general preparation in political science provides the necessary background for entry-level jobs in nonprofit management. In addition, some schools offer courses that specifically address issues related to nonprofit administration. These may be offered within a political science department, or through a school of business but open to students from other disciplines, including political science.

For example, Regent University in Virginia offers master's level courses in a "nonprofit management track" designed to prepare students for leadership roles in the nonprofit sector. Students prepare for work in churches, educational institutions, or other nonprofit organizations. Course offerings include "Managing Nonprofit Organizations," "Leadership," and "Leadership: Personality and Communication."

Another program worth noting is offered by The New School through its Robert J. Milano School of Management and Urban Policy. This college offers a master of science degree in nonprofit management. The New School is located in New York City where, according to school officials, one in seven people works in the nonprofit sector.

For information, write to

MS Program in Nonprofit Management
Milano Graduate School
The New School
66 Fifth Avenue
New York, NY 10011

Even if you gain an entry-level position, you'll find that working in the nonprofit sector often requires special knowledge, gained either in college, on the job, or through a combination of the two. Here are some common topics covered by managers in nonprofit settings:

Annual fund strategies

Basic fund-raising principles

Basic grantsmanship

Building endowments

Corporate and foundation fund-raising

Direct mail fund-raising

Effective proposal development

Ethics of fund-raising

Grant writing basics

Managing volunteers

Office management techniques

Organizing capital campaigns

Planned-giving programs

Principles of grant management

Public relations strategies

Strategic planning

Using computers in fund-raising

Working with boards

Writing for development

Fortunately, many of these skills are consistent with the kind of knowledge and interest levels typically demonstrated by political science students and graduates. With additional training and job experience, the typical political science major can readily adapt to the work performed in nonprofit organizations.

STRATEGIES FOR FINDING JOBS

There is no single method for finding jobs in the nonprofit sector. One place to start is your college's career placement office. Be alert for campus visitations by representatives of nonprofit organizations, as well as for postings of job openings with such groups. Then apply for any that interest you.

The classified sections of major newspapers also include ads for jobs with nonprofit organizations. Newspapers published in smaller cites will include ads for local job openings, but you'll need to consult major papers such as the *New York Times* and *Washington Post* for regional or national openings.

You can also contact organizations directly and request information on job openings and how you might apply. Some organizations now include such information on-line; you need only check out their sites on the World Wide Web.

Perhaps the best sources of job information are publications targeted specifically to those who are already employed in the nonprofit sector or who have other direct ties such as service on boards of directors.

For example, the *Chronicle of Philanthropy*, published twenty-four times a year, includes an exhaustive list of job openings in nonprofit organizations in each issue. In addition, the *Chronicle* is a solid source of information about events and trends in the nonprofit world. It covers fund-raising ideas and techniques, reports on tax and court rulings, and provides information about conferences and other professional development opportunities, among other topics.

For subscription information, write to

Chronicle of Philanthropy
P.O. Box 1989
Marion, OH 43305

While the *Chronicle of Philanthropy* focuses on private giving, a publication that is more general is *The Nonprofit Times*. This newspaper bills itself as "The Leading Business Publication for Nonprofit Management." Along with news of interest to those working in nonprofit organizations, each issue includes a number of job openings.

For information, write to

The Nonprofit Times
240 Cedar Knolls Road, Suite 318
Cedar Knolls, NJ 07927

Another publication that lists job openings in the nonprofit world is *Community Jobs*, published in Washington, D.C. Appearing ten times per year, this publication includes a large number of job announcements in every issue. For subscription information, write to

Community Jobs
1001 Connecticut Avenue NW
Washington, DC 20036

An on-line job service which you might want to check out is

The Community Career Center
Enterprise, Inc.
2160 W. Charleston
Las Vegas, NV 89102
http://www.nonprofitjobs.org

THE NATIONAL SOCIETY OF FUND RAISING EXECUTIVES

The National Society of Fund Raising Executives (NSFRE), headquartered in Alexandria, Virginia, is a good source of information about the fund-raising profession. This progressive organization has more than 17,000 members in chapters located throughout North America. Members hold a variety of jobs in nonprofit and charitable organizations.

An especially noteworthy service of this association is its certification programs. Through its Certified Fund Raising Executive (CFRE) and Advanced Certified Fund Raising Executive (ACFRE) programs, the association provides certification that professionals have met certain standards for excellence in fund-raising. These credentials can be used to enhance other educational backgrounds after one has established some experience in the field. Potentially, a person with a political science background and a CFRE designation might fare better in advancing on the job or seeking new jobs than one without this respected designation.

The NSFRE also provides a variety of educational opportunities. Among these are regular offerings such as the annual International Conference on Fund-Raising, the Executive Leadership Institute, the Survey Course on Fund Raising, and the First Course in Fund Raising.

For more information about this organization, contact

National Society of Fund Raising Executives
1101 King Street, Suite 700
Alexandria, VA 22314

WORKING CONDITIONS

Working conditions in nonprofit management vary widely. Typically, standard office settings can be expected. Surroundings might range from a cubicle with a desk and phone to a large, attractive office. The smaller the organization or the less experienced the worker, the more likely that work settings will be simple.

Aside from the basics of office locations and furnishings, one advantage of the nonprofit setting is that flexibility is common in when and how work may be performed. For example, employers may allow some degree of "telecommuting," where staff work out of their homes instead of reporting to an office. Flex time, where workers are expected to work a minimum number of hours but may adjust schedules according to their own personal preferences, is also offered by some employers.

Work settings may also vary if travel or case work is required. For instance, a program officer for a foundation may travel to locations where grants have been awarded and review the progress made possible through grant funding. For a community foundation this might mean driving across town and visiting a shelter for the homeless. For a program officer with the Ford Foundation it could mean flying to Bolivia to review progress in establishing a preschool program for disadvantaged children.

SERVICE EXPERIENCES

The Toughest Job You Ever Loved?

If you want to work hard, earn very little money, but gain invaluable experience, consider joining the Peace Corps. Certainly this avenue isn't for everyone, but it can be a great experience for political science graduates who want to serve others while gaining some valuable life experience.

For more information about the Peace Corps, contact national headquarters or one of the regional recruiting offices listed below.

Peace Corps National Headquarters

Peace Corps
1990 K Street NW
Washington, DC 20526

Peace Corps Recruiting Offices

For Alabama, Florida, Georgia, Mississippi, South Carolina, Tennessee:

Peace Corps Recruiting Office
100 Alabama Street 2R70
Atlanta, GA 30303

For Massachusetts, Vermont, Rhode Island, Maine, New Hampshire:

Peace Corps Recruiting Office
Tip O'Neill Federal Building
10 Causeway Street, Room 450
Boston, MA 02222

For Illinois, Indiana, Ohio, Michigan:

Peace Corps Recruiting Office
Xerox Center
55 W. Monroe Street, Suite 450
Chicago, IL 60603

For New Mexico, Oklahoma, Louisiana, Texas, Arkansas:

Peace Corps Recruiting Office
207 S. Houston Street, Room 527
Dallas, TX 75202

For Maryland, District of Columbia, North Carolina, West Virginia, Virginia:

Peace Corps Recruiting Office
1400 Wilson Boulevard, Suite 400
Arlington, VA 22209

For Colorado, Montana, South Dakota, North Dakota, Utah, Wyoming:

Peace Corps Recruiting Office
1999 Broadway, Suite 2205
Denver, CO 80202-3050

For Arizona and Southern California:

Peace Corps Recruiting Office
11000 Wilshire Boulevard., Room 8104
West Los Angeles, CA 90024

For Minnesota and Wisconsin:

Peace Corps Recruiting Office
330 2nd Avenue South
Minneapolis, MN 55401

For New York, New Jersey, Connecticut, Pennsylvania:

Peace Corps Recruiting Office
6 World Trade Center, Room 611
New York, NY 10048

For Alaska, Idaho, Montana, Oregon, Washington:

Peace Corps Recruiting Office
2001 6th Avenue, Room 1776
Seattle, WA 98121

For Hawaii, Northern California, Nevada:

Peace Corps Recruiting Office
211 Main Street, Room 533
San Francisco, CA 94105

AmeriCorps

While the Peace Corps may be the most famous service outreach program, it is by no means the only one. You can gain similar experiences without working in a third-world country. A domestic program that might be of interest to political science majors interested in broadening their experience is Ameri-Corps. This is a national service program that places participants in community-based positions. Some participants join before attending college, while others participate after completing their degrees, and some use the program as a break from college. Service projects range from working in schools to rebuilding homes damaged by floods or hurricanes. In exchange for a year of service, AmeriCorps volunteers receive a living stipend, health insurance, and an education voucher that can be used to pay back student loans or for tuition for additional college studies.

For more information, contact

AmeriCorps
Corporation for National Service
1201 New York Avenue NW
Washington, DC 20525

RELATED OCCUPATIONS

Many of the skills involved in nonprofit management can be applied in other career areas. Skills such as planning, organizing, communicating, and supervising others can be applied in small businesses, large corporations, and other settings. Following are some representative job titles for related career areas.

Account executive	Marketing director
Director, quality assurance	Office manager
Hospital administrator	Sales manager
Human resource manager	Teacher
Labor relations supervisor	Technical editor
Management consultant	

PROFESSIONAL ASSOCIATIONS FOR NONPROFIT EXECUTIVES, MANAGERS, AND RELATED PROFESSIONALS

American Society of Association Executives
1575 I Street NW
Washington, DC 20005
Members/Purpose: Promotes and supports excellence and professionalism among executives of trade associations, individual membership societies, voluntary organizations, and other not-for-profit associations.
Training: Annual conference as well as special conferences and symposia.
Journal/Publication: *Association Management* magazine.

National Council of Nonprofit Associations
1001 Connecticut Avenue NW
Washington, DC 20036

Members/Purpose: Coordinating group for thirty nonprofit organizations. Provides information, advocacy, and professional development opportunities.
Training: Annual conference and biennial regional membership meetings.
Journal/Publication: *State Tax Trends for Nonprofits.*

National Society of Fund Raising Executives (NSFRE):
1101 King Street, Suite 700
Alexandria, VA 22314
Members/Purpose: Serves individuals responsible for generating philanthropic support for a variety of nonprofit, charitable organizations.
Training: Annual conference, courses on fund-raising, certification program.
Journal/Publication: Quarterly journal, *Advancing Philanthropy.*

Nonprofit Management Association
315 W. Ninth Street
Los Angeles, CA 90015
Members/Purpose: Serves individuals who manage nonprofit groups or provide management or technical assistance.
Training: Annual conference.
Journal/Publication: *NMA Bulletin Board.*

APPENDIX

ADDITIONAL RESOURCES

ABA Journal
750 N. Lake Shore Drive
Chicago, IL 60611

ASCUS Annual
Association for School, College and University Staffing
1600 Dodge Avenue, S-33
Evanston, IL 60201

American Journal of Political Science
University of Wisconsin Press
114 N. Murray Street
Madison, WI 53715

American Political Science Review
303 South Kedzie Hall
Michigan State University
East Lansing, MI 48824

American Politics Quarterly
Sage Publications
2455 Teller Road
Thousand Oaks, CA 91320

American Review of Politics
University of Central Arkansas Press
Conway, AR 72032

America's Teachers: An Introduction to Education
Addison-Wesley Publishing
1 Jacobs Way
Reading, MA 01867

Association Management
American Society of Association Executives
1575 I Street NW
Washington, DC 20005

Audio Video Market Place
R.R. Bowker Company
245 W. 17th Street
New York, NY 10011

Braddock's Federal-State-Local Government Directory
Braddock Communications
909 N. Washington Street
Alexandria, VA 22314

Campaigns and Elections
1511 K Street NW
Washington, DC 20005

Canadian Journal of Political Science
Canadian Political Science Association
1 Steward Street
Ottawa, Ontario
Canada K1N 6H7

The Career Guide: Dun's Employment Opportunities Directory
Dun & Bradstreet Information Services
899 Eaton Avenue
Bethlehem, PA 18025

Careers and the Study of Political Science
American Political Science Association
1527 New Hampshire Avenue NW
Washington, DC 20036

Careers Encyclopedia
NTC/Contemporary Publishing Group, Inc.
4255 W. Touhy Avenue
Lincolnwood, IL 60646

Careers in Government
NTC/Contemporary Publishing Group, Inc.
4255 W. Touhy Avenue
Lincolnwood, IL 60646

Careers in State and Local Government
Garrett Park Press
Garrett Park, MD 20896

Careers for Dreamers and Doers: A Guide to Management Careers in the Nonprofit Sector
The Foundation Center
79 Fifth Avenue
New York, NY 10003

Careers for Legal Eagles and Other Law-and-Order Types
NTC/Contemporary Publishing Group, Inc.
4255 W. Touhy Avenue
Lincolnwood, IL 60646

Changing Patterns in State Government Careers
University of Michigan Press
839 Greene Street
P.O. Box 1104
Ann Arbor, MI 48106

The Chronicle of Higher Education
1255 Twenty-Third Street NW
Washington, DC 20037

Careers in Education
NTC/Contemporary Publishing Group, Inc.
4255 W. Touhy Avenue
Lincolnwood, IL 60646

Careers in Teaching
Rosen Publishing
29 E. 21st Street
New York, NY 10010

Careers for Political Scientists
Canadian Political Science Association
1 Steward Street
Ottawa, Ontario
Canada K1N 6H7

The Chicago Tribune
435 N. Michigan Avenue
Chicago, IL 60611

Common Cause Magazine
2030 M Street NW
Washington, DC 20036

Community Jobs
1001 Connecticut Avenue NW
Washington, DC 20036

Comparative Political Studies
Sage Publications
2455 Teller Road
Thousand Oaks, CA 91320

Comparative Politics
City University of New York
33 W. 42nd Street
New York, NY 10036

The Complete Guide to Public Employment
Impact Publications
4580 Sunshine Court
Woodbridge, VA 22191

County Executive Directory
Carroll Publishing
1058 Thomas Jefferson Street NW
Washington, DC 20077

Current Jobs for Graduates
Plymouth Publishing, Inc.
P.O. Box 40550
Washington, DC 20016

Directory of City Policy Officials
National League of Cities
1301 Pennsylvania Avenue
Washington, DC 20004

Directory of Directories
Gale Research, Inc.
P.O. Box 33477
Detroit, MI 48232

DISCOVER
American College Testing
Educational Services Division
P.O. Box 168
Iowa City, IA 52244

Doing Well by Doing Good: The Complete Guide to Careers in the Nonprofit Sector
The Taft Group
645 Groswold Street
Detroit, MI 48226

Earning a Ph.D. in Political Science
American Political Science Association
1527 New Hampshire Avenue NW
Washington, DC 20036

EEO Bimonthly
CASS Communications
1800 Sherman Avenue, Suite 300
Evanston, IL 60201

Federal Career Opportunities
Gordon Press Publishers
P.O. Box 459
Bowling Green Station
New York, NY 10004

Federal Jobs Digest
Breakthrough Publications
P.O. Box 594
Millwood, NY 10546

Federal Law Related Careers
Federal Reports
1010 Vermont Avenue NW
Washington, DC 20005

Foreign Service Journal
2101 E Street NW
Washington, DC 20037

Good Works: A Guide to Careers in Social Change
Barricade Books
150 Fifth Avenue, Suite 700
New York, NY 10011

Government Executive
1501 M Street NW
Washington, DC 20005

Government Job Finder
Planning Communications
7215 Oak Avenue
River Forest, IL 60305

The Handbook of Private Schools
Porter Sargent Publishers
11 Beacon Street, Suite 1400
Boston, MA 02108

The Harvard College Guide to Careers in Government and Politics
Harvard University
79 Garden Street
Cambridge, MA 02138

Independent School
National Association of Independent Schools
1620 L Street NW
Washington, DC 20036

Index of Majors and Graduate Degrees
College Board Publications
P.O. Box 886
New York, NY 10101

Instructor **Magazine**
555 Broadway
New York, NY 10012

Job Hotlines USA
Career Communications Inc.
P.O. Box 169
Harleyville, PA 19438

The Job Source Series
2000 L Street NW
Washington, DC 20036

Journal of Politics
Southern Political Science Association
Department of Political Science
University of North Carolina
Chapel Hill, North Carolina 27599

The Lawyers Weekly
75 Clegg Road
Markham, Ontario
L6G IA1 Canada

The Legal Career Guide: From Law Student to Lawyer
American Bar Association
750 N. Lake Shore Drive
Chicago, IL 60611

Legislative Studies Quarterly
Comparative Legislative Research Center
334 Schaeffer
University of Iowa
Iowa City, IA 52242

The Los Angeles Times
Times Mirror Square
Los Angeles, CA 90053

Master of Public Administration
National Association of Schools of Public Affairs and Administration
1120 G Street NW
Washington, DC 20005

Municipal Executive Directory
Carroll Publishing Co.
1058 Thomas Jefferson Street NW
Washington, DC 20077

The Municipal Yearbook
International City Management Association
777 N. Capitol Street NE
Washington, DC 20002

National Business Employment Weekly
Dow Jones & Company
P.O. Box 300
Princeton, NJ 08543

National Center for Education Statistics
America's Teachers: Profile of a Profession
U.S. Department of Education
Office of Educational Research and Improvement
Washington, DC 20208

National Directory of Internships
National Society for Internships and Experiential Education
3509 Haworth Drive, Suite 207
Raleigh, NC 27609

The New York Times
229 W. 43rd Street
New York, NY 10036

Non-Profit Job Finder
Planning/Communications
7215 Oak Avenue
River Forest, IL 60305

The Non-Profit Times
240 Cedar Knolls Road, Suite 318
Cedar Knolls, NJ 07927

The National Law Journal
345 Park Avenue S.
New York, NY 10010

National Standards for Civics and Government
Center for Civic Education
5146 Douglas Fir Road
Calabaras, CA 91302

Nonlegal Careers for Lawyers in the Private Sector
American Bar Association
750 N. Lake Shore Drive
Chicago, IL 60611

Non-Profits and Education Job Finder
Planning/Communications
7215 Oak Avenue
River Front, IL 60305

Occupational Outlook Handbook
Occupational Outlook Quarterly
U.S. Department of Labor
Bureau of Labor Statistics
Washington, DC 20212

Opportunities in Federal Government Careers
NTC/Contemporary Publishing Group, Inc.
4255 W. Touhy Avenue
Lincolnwood, IL 60646

Opportunities in State and Local Government Careers
NTC/Contemporary Publishing Group, Inc.
4255 W. Touhy Avenue
Lincolnwood, IL 60646

Patterson's American Education
Educational Directories Inc.
P.O. Box 199
Mount Prospect, IL 60056

Political Science Quarterly
Academy of Political Science
475 Riverside Drive, Suite 1274
New York, NY 10015

Philanthropy Journal
5 W. Hargett Street, Suite 805
Raleigh, NC 27601

Philanthropic Digest
P.O. Box 325
Clinton, NY 13323

Planning
American Planning Association
122 S. Michigan Avenue
Chicago, IL 60603

Policy Studies Journal
Policy Studies Review
University of Illinois
361 Lincoln Hall
Urbana, IL 61801

Public Administration Review
American Society for Public Administration
1120 G Street NW, Suite 700
Washington, DC 20005

Public Affairs Report
University of California at Berkeley
Institute of Governmental Studies
109 Moses Hall
Berkeley, CA 94720

Public Opinion Quarterly
University of Chicago Press
5720 S. Woodlawn Avenue
Chicago, IL 60637

PS: Political Science and Politics
American Political Science Association
1527 New Hampshire Avenue NW
Washington, DC 20036

Regional, State and Local Organizations
Gale Research, Inc.
P.O. Box 33477
River Forest, IL 60305

Resumes for Government Careers
NTC/Contemporary Publishing Group, Inc.
4255 W. Touhy Avenue
Lincolnwood, IL 60646

State and Local Government Review
Carl Vinson Institute of Government
University of Georgia
201 N. Milledge Avenue
Athens, GA 30602

State Executive Directory
Carroll Publishing Co.
1058 Thomas Jefferson Street NW
Washington, DC 20077

State Government Research Directory
Gale Research, Inc.
P.O. Box 33477
River Forest, IL 60305

Storming Washington: An Intern's Guide to National Government
American Political Science Association
1527 New Hampshire Avenue NW
Washington, DC 20036

Student Lawyer
American Bar Association
750 N. Lake Shore Drive
Chicago, IL 60611

Women and Politics
The Ha'p'orth Press
Political Science Department
State University of West Georgia
Carrollton, GA 30118

Women's Political Times
Women's Political Caucus
1211 Connecticut Avenue NW
Washington, DC 20036

The World Almanac of U.S. Politics
World Almanac Books
1 International Boulevard
Mahwah, NJ 07495

VGM's Handbook of Government and Public Service Careers
NTC/Contemporary Publishing Group, Inc.
4255 W. Touhy Avenue
Lincolnwood, IL 60646

The Washington Post
1150 15th Street NW
Washington, DC 20071

Working for Your Uncle: The Complete Guide to Finding a Job in the Federal Government
Breakthrough Publications
310 N. Highland Avenue
Ossining, NY 10562

INDEX